4/10

HIST

Scheduling the Heavens

the story of

EDMOND HALLEY

Scheduling the Heavens

the story of

EDMOND HALLEY

Mary Virginia Fox

MORGAN REYNOLDS

PUBLISHING

Greensboro, North Carolina

Profiles
IN SCIENCE

Robert Boyle
Rosalind Franklin
Ibn al-Haytham
Edmond Halley
Marie Curie
Caroline Herschel

SCHEDULING THE HEAVENS
THE STORY OF EDMOND HALLEY

Copyright © 2007 by Mary Virginia Fox

Library of Congress Cataloging-in-Publication Data

Fox, Mary Virginia.
   Scheduling the heavens : the story of Edmond Halley / by Mary Virginia
Fox. -- 1st ed.
      p. cm. -- (Profiles in science)
   Includes bibliographical references and index.
   ISBN-13: 978-1-59935-021-9 (alk. paper)
   ISBN-10: 1-59935-021-1 (alk. paper)
   1.   Halley, Edmond, 1656-1742. 2.   Astronomers--Great
Britain--Biography.
   3. Astronomy--England--History. 4. Royal Society (Great Britain) I.
Title.
   QB36.H25F69 2006
   520.92--dc22
   [B]
                                        2006031269

Printed in the United States of America
First Edition

To my sister, Leila Merrell Foster, JD, PhD, also a writer

Contents

Edmond Halley

one

AMBITION
AND GENIUS

Edmond Halley observed his first comet at age twenty-five, while sailing across the English Channel to Paris in 1681. The trip was part of the young astronomer's Grand Tour of Europe, a customary rite of passage for a gentleman's education. When the ship landed, Halley hurried to the observatories of the best-known astronomers in France, to see the brightest comet anyone alive had witnessed. He found the equipment inferior to what he used in England, however, and the sky was overcast. But Halley, who would go on to dedicate his entire life to investigating natural phenomena, and to studying the schedule and orbit of comets—the most

The appearance of Halley's comet has invoked fear in people for centuries.
(Courtesy of the Granger Collection)

unpredictable of all the celestial objects—did not have to wait long to observe another one.

In November 1682, Halley and many others in Europe began watching a comet that first appeared as a smudge of light moving across the sky. As the days passed, Halley could discern its bright head and the streaks of light that trailed behind it, like strands of flowing hair.

He took detailed measurements of the comet, writing down the dates and times of his observations, and its daily location in relation to the stars. Using these recordings, a future astronomer would be able to plot an exact graph of the path the comet had taken.

Soon the comet was visible without a telescope—it got so close that many people feared it was on a course to plunge to Earth. Halley believed otherwise: his observations and calculations indicated it was not moving on a collision course. But despite the abundance of figures and notes, Halley's notebook contained as many questions as answers. His skills had not developed enough to understand how the gravitational pull of planets altered the orbit and speed of comets as they passed. But he knew that someday it would be possible to gain a clearer understanding of how gravity worked, and how the planets and other celestial bodies traveled.

It would take him twenty years to work out the schedule of the Great Comet of 1682, and predict its return. But in the intervening years, Halley would become one of the most productive and brilliant scientists in Europe. He would also become the comet's greatest ambassador. In this role, he proved key to making sure that perhaps the greatest single work of science ever written saw the light of day.

Edmond Halley was born on October 29, 1656, in Haggerston, England, which was then just to the north of London, to Anne Robinson Halley and Edmond Halley Sr. There is little record of his mother, who died in 1672. The strongest influence on Halley was his father who, although not of noble birth, had acquired a sizable estate by virtue of his shrewdness and hard work. He had started a business making soap and salt, and people were just beginning to believe that cleanliness was a virtue. His soap was made from boiling the carcasses of dead animals. The process produced a terrible stench. Luckily for the Halleys, the soap-making factory was in the poor part of the city, far from the family's home. Salt was in high demand as a meat preserver, in an era long

When the bubonic plague hit England in 1664, more than 25 percent of London's residents died.

before refrigeration. Sailors ate a diet heavy in salted products, and keeping sailors fed was critical to a seafaring nation like England. The English navy was its front line of defense, and the tiny island nation depended on a large commercial fleet to carry on trade.

The elder Halley had also invested his profits in real estate, and the rents along with the income from two profitable businesses, provided a comfortable lifestyle for his family. He owned both a house in town on Winchester Street, and a country house at Haggerston. Edward was born at the country home outside of London. Several years after Edmond's arrival, a sister, Kathleen, was born. She died while still an infant. The Halleys also had a boy named Humphrey who did not live to adulthood.

Infant mortality and early death in general was painfully common in the sixteenth century. Although science was developing quickly, and new empirically supported explanations of how the physical world worked were being revealed every year, medical practice had not advanced much beyond the tried and not-so-true medieval methods. No one really knew what caused illness, and neither bacteria nor germs had been identified yet.

When the bubonic plague, called the Black Death, swept through London and other parts of England in 1664 and 1665, it killed thousands of people—more than 25 percent of the population of London alone. Because the disease was almost always fatal, anyone able to escape to the less-populated countryside did so in order to lessen the danger of contracting the plague. (One of the people who fled to the countryside was Cambridge student Isaac Newton, who took advantage of his time away from school to make many of the scientific breakthroughs that would make him famous later.) No one realized the plague was spread by fleas living on the rats that swarmed through the tenement districts of the big city.

Soon after the devastation of the plague another tragedy hit London, one that created a crisis in the Halley family. During the 1666 Great Fire of London, thousands of homes and buildings, most built with

The Black Death, as the bubonic plague was called, was caused by the fleas carried on rats.

wooden timbers and thatched roofs, were destroyed. The elder Halley had invested heavily in London rental property and lost much of his investment. A prudent man, he realized that while fire could burn buildings the land they stood on still had value. Gradually the city began to rebuild, and cleaner, more sanitary communities evolved. Halley now could charge higher rents for new buildings, which helped him recoup his financial losses.

In 1666 London was devastated by a fire that destroyed thousands of homes.

For young Edmond, it was a time of rapid change. The Renaissance had come and gone, but had left in its wake a new spirit of inquiry. Systematic science was still new, and many of the educated elite spent their leisure time pursuing it. More than a thirst for knowledge drove this interest in science and technology. New trade routes had opened across Asia, as well as to Africa, and new colonies were being established in North and South America. Better navigational tools were needed to more safely make the voyages, and new minerals, plants and even species were being discovered and brought back to England every year. The world was getting smaller, and knowledge was more valuable than ever before.

Edmond also came of age during an era of great political change. After years of civil war, the government was

Oliver Cromwell controlled the government of England from 1649 to 1660.

controlled from 1649 to 1660 by a protectorate dominated by the commoner Oliver Cromwell, a strict Puritan. The monarchy was restored in 1660 when Charles II assumed the throne. The king's father, Charles I, had been beheaded in 1649, only a few years before Edmond was born. The restoration of the monarchy was beneficial to Halley's future because it reinstated royal patronage to the arts and sciences.

In the midst of all this political turmoil, Edmond's father planned his son's future carefully. He provided young Halley with all the educational advantages he could. Even before beginning formal education Halley was taught to read, write, and do mathematics. Then he was sent to St. Paul's School, which was founded in 1509 and is still in existence today. St. Paul's had originally been created by the Catholic Church to provide education for poor boys. However, by the time Edmond enrolled, the Church of England had replaced the Catholic Church as the official state church, and the cost of enrollment at St. Paul's had increased to a level that only wealthy families could afford.

The school's curriculum included the traditional focus on Latin, Greek, and Hebrew, but Halley also took lessons in mathematics, navigation, geometry, trigonometry, algebra, and astronomy. As a young man, Halley was slender with brown hair and eyes. He applied himself diligently to his studies, but he was also lively with a great sense of humor and popular with his classmates. He liked to talk, whether it was to give reports of his scientific work or just to gather a group of friends around to have fun. He was chosen captain of the student body at age fifteen.

Halley impressed both his teachers and schoolmates with his intellect. One of Halley's contemporaries, Anthony Wood, wrote of Halley:

> He not only excelled in every branch of classical learning, but he was particularly taken notice of for the extraordinary advances he made at the same time in the Mathematicks. In so much, that he seems not only to have acquired almost a masterly skill in both plain and spherical Trigonometry, but to be well acquainted with the science of Navigation, and to have made great progress in Astronomy before he was removed to Oxford.

Halley later wrote that "from my tenderest youth I gave myself over to the consideration of Astronomy" and that science gave him "so much pleasure as is impossible to explain to anyone who has not experienced it." Halley was encouraged to pursue his interest in astronomy by one of his professors at St. Paul's, Thomas Gale. Prior to coming to St. Paul's School, Gale had served as head of Greek studies and language at Oxford. A distinguished scholar, he was a man of varied interests, including the "new philosophy of science." Gale recognized Halley's academic excellence and gave him special instruction in Greek and encouraged him to continue his education at Oxford.

two

NIGHT SKY

From his student days, Halley spent so much time studying the heavens that it was later said that if a star dropped from the charts he would recognize the change immediately. Always ready to encourage his precocious son, Edmond Halley Sr. even had a twenty-four-foot long telescope built for his son.

Halley did not restrict his work to astronomy. He was interested in all aspects of the natural world. At age sixteen, he began trying to measure the difference between the exact location of what we call the North Pole and the place where a magnetic compass points to as north. This particular anomaly was not conclusively explained until modern times, when it was attributed to a shift of the molten iron core deep inside Earth.

The Earth's Magnetic Field

The Earth is like a gigantic magnet. At the center of the earth lies a molten, metallic, iron-rich core. The outer portion of this core is semiliquid, rather than solid. It is also believed that the core is slowly spinning. Metals in the core have many loosely bound electrons, and these particles can conduct electricity.

The geographic location of the North Pole is where the imaginary lines of longitude meet, but that seldom coincides with the point of greatest magnetic attraction on an ordinary compass.

1672 was an exciting year for Halley. He was ready to enter college. But it was also a time of deep sadness. Shortly before he left for Oxford University his mother died. The cause of her death is unknown. Records tell us only that she was buried in a small town called Barking in Essex, presumably where her own parents lived.

It must have been hard for a widowed father to see his son and only surviving child leave home, but Halley Sr. had always encouraged Edmond to seek further education. Halley was sixteen when he traveled alone to Oxford University to enter Queen's College. Not many young men, and no women, went to college in those days. Most who attended planned to either become a teacher or a minister, who studied Biblical history and the writings of ancient cultures. Higher learning was reserved for an elite group of individuals, and Edmond Halley fit perfectly into that classification.

At Oxford, a student was placed under the supervision of one professor who set the student's course of study and considered his queries and discussions one-on-one. Halley sought out professors who could give him further training

Halley attended Queen's College at Oxford University in England.

in astronomy. One professor, Anthony Wood, said about Halley: "He had at this time perfectly learned the use of the celestial globe and could make a complete dial." As a practical astronomer, Halley had already begun to use his telescope to study the position of stars and planets.

Navigation Instruments

In the Middle Ages, sailors relied on the astrolabe, a handheld disc of metal suspended by a small ring. It was marked off in 360 degrees—the number of degrees in a circle—and had a ruler to measure the height from the horizon. It was used to show how the sky looks at a specific place at a given time.

The sextant was invented in 1731. The scale of a sextant has a length of one-sixth of a full circle, or sixty degrees, hence the sextant's name ("sex" is the Latin prefix for "six"). A common use of the sextant is to sight the sun at noon to find one's latitude, which provides much better precision than the astrolabe. A sextant is made up of two arms set at an angle of sixty degrees and a curved scale between. A sextant's view merges two views: one view is of the sky, through the mirrors at the eyepiece, and the other view is of the horizon. You take a sighting by adjusting a screw until the lower

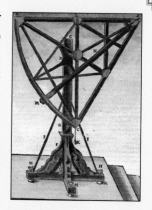

edge of an image of a celestial body touches the horizon.

The quadrant was used to find latitude by measuring the angle between the North Star or the sun and the horizon. The quadrant got its name because it could measure angles of up to ninety degrees, one quarter of a circle. It was made of wood or metal and got its

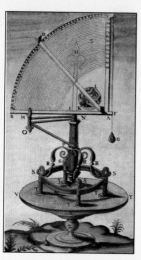

name because it was shaped in the form of a quarter of a circle. There were sights along one of the radial arms. When it was used, the quadrant was held with the arc straight down. A plumb line was suspended at a right angle. The sailor held the quadrant with the arc straight down and aligned the sights at the sun or star. Once the sights were aligned he would hold the plumb line against the scale on the face of the quadrant and read off the altitude. Two pinhole sights along one edge of the quadrant allowed the user to line up the sights. A plumb line suspended from the apex of the quadrant was weighted to hang straight down. The sailor would tilt the quadrant and use the sights to fix on the sun or a star and then determine the altitude by reading where the plumb line intersected with a degree scale engraved along the radial edge of the quadrant.

Students and teachers at Oxford liked and respected Halley, and he excelled and enjoyed the acclaim. But, even before graduating, he became restless. New discoveries were being made, and he was impatient to become a part of them.

Insatiably curious, ambitious, and eager to get going on the newest project, to make the next discovery, Halley was sometimes criticized for having too many interests, and for being too easily bored with any one subject to make truly profound discoveries. If pulled in too many directions, he would prove no different than other men of his time. The greatest of his contemporaries, Sir Isaac Newton, whose work shattered most of the old assumptions about the physical laws of the universe, devoted much more of his working life to studying theology and alchemy than scientific research.

The one topic Halley made his own was the study of comets, or more precisely the orbits of comets. He spent little if any time trying to understand what comets were made of, for example, or how hot or cold they were. He wanted to know their schedules. Comets were unpredictable, suddenly appearing on the horizon, growing brighter over a period of days, their thin tails either in the front or the back, or just as mysteriously disappearing. Most saw comets as omens, usually bad ones. Ancient texts were full of stories of the comets appearing at climatic moments, such as the assassination of Julius Caesar.

In 1675, King Charles II of England established a new observatory at Greenwich. Sir Christopher Wren, a highly respected mathematician, astronomer, and architect, built the observatory. The king appointed John Flamsteed as the first Royal Astronomer.

One of Flamsteed's first tasks was to study map making. Longitude presented the biggest problem in navigation. It

In 1675 John Flamsteed was appointed as the first Royal Astronomer by King Charles II. (Courtesy of Heritage Images)

was quite easy to determine latitude. On a clear night, sailors could use a compass to locate the north celestial pole or observe the comparative altitude of a star or sun or moon above the horizon and, based upon the time of day, calculate how far north or south they were from the equator. But longitude was a more difficult matter because it cannot be determined from the horizon. It is the imaginary line from the South Pole to the North Pole.

Establishment of the Greenwich Meridian

An International Meridian Conference was held in Washington, D. C., in October 1884. Representatives from twenty-five countries attended. It had become obvious the world needed a zero meridian for determining time and longitude. The difficulty came in deciding where it should be. After a protracted debate, Greenwich, England was chosen, primarily because it was already being used as the prime meridian by more than 70 percent of the world's ships. Another stated reason was that James Cook and other English sailors created the first accurate charts of the world in the eighteenth century, and these charts referred to the zero meridian at Greenwich, and chronometers could find their longitude set to Greenwich Mean Time.

In 1884 Greenwich, England, was made the official place for zero meridian for determining time and longitude.

The Greenwich Meridian is designated zero degrees longitude. Working outward from zero degrees, it was possible to draw other longitude lines one degree apart.

Halley had other projects to do before he worked on longitude and navigation. During his last year as an undergraduate at Oxford, Halley became puzzled by some of the planetary positions given in the published tables. These tables were published to locate a planet at any time of the year. They had been computed mathematically but had not been verified by observation. Halley set out to verify some of the tables by making his own observations at home, sometimes working with a fellow student, Charles Bouchar. He soon discovered that many of the actual positions did not match the published tables.

Bouchar, who was older than Halley, had previously written to Royal Astronomer Flamsteed to ask a question about a problem he was trying to solve and had received a courteous reply. Halley decided to write his own letter to Flamsteed. He began by flattering the Royal Astronomer, mentioning the kindness Flamsteed had extended to Bouchar. Halley explained his love for the field of astronomy and described his precise observations. He explained that he used a small telescope fitted to his quadrant and could "confide to one minute without error by means of the telescopicall sights and skrew for the subdivision of my Quadrant . . ." This was no idle boast. Halley's calculations were as accurate as any that could be made with the telescopes available in his time.

Halley went on to point out that the published positions of the planets Jupiter and Saturn were erroneous. He softened this brash claim with a request: if Flamsteed himself had "observed anything of the like nature in Saturn, I beg you would communicate it." In other words, Halley wanted the Royal Astronomer to confirm his own observations. Then he asked for permission to visit Flamsteed in Greenwich to discuss his work in person.

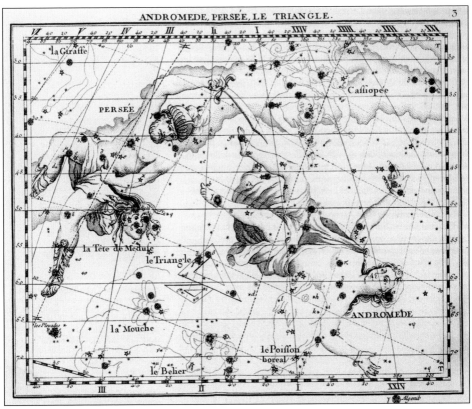

A decorative star map from Flamsteed's British History of the Heavens

Halley's letter also described the observations he made of a lunar eclipse on the first of January 1675. He had timed the position of the bright star Pollux at the exact moment when the whole disk of the moon was obscured by the earth's shadow, as well as the moment when the moon began to emerge from the eclipse. By comparing the angles he charted from this triangulation of the earth, moon and the star Pollux during the time of the eclipse, Halley showed the published stellar tables to be wrong. Although the measurements to the moon changed as the shadow of the earth crossed the path, he observed that the far-off image of the star did not.

After making multiple sightings during the eclipse, Halley transcribed his figures in his notebook. He drew lines converging on Pollux and spent hours doing calculations. In the end, his measurements revealed the position of the star to be a degree or two different from the location given on sky maps then in use. This may not seem like a momentous discovery, but accuracy was the goal, and Halley worried that other inconsistencies might exist in the star charts of the day.

Halley mentioned to Flamsteed that he intended to observe a conjunction of Mars and the moon twelve days later. A conjunction is the moment when the moon blots out the sight of Mars, and Halley hoped that Flamsteed would also be watching to verify his findings. In his own words, Halley refers to his previous observations "as a specimen of my Astronomical endeavours I send you, being ambitious in the honour of being known to you, of which if you shall deem me worthy I shall account myself exceedingly happy in the enjoyment of the acquaintance of so illustrious and deserving a person as your self."

Flamsteed's letter of reply is lost, but it must have been positive. Halley was invited to come to the observatory in Greenwich to check his own observations on the more elaborate scientific equipment owned by the Royal Astronomer.

Flamsteed was impressed with the young man, who was ten years younger. He agreed to publish some of Halley's figures along with his own in the scientific journal *Philosophical Transactions*. This gave a boost to Halley's prestige to have his work recognized by the elite members of his profession. The two developed a close collaboration, at least for the time being.

Kepler's Laws of Planetary Motion

Johannes Kepler

Johannes Kepler was a critical figure in the understanding of planetary motion. His greatest achievements are his three laws of planetary motion.

The first law established that the path of the planets' orbits was not circular, but an ellipse, with the center of the sun being located at one focus.

The second law, which describes the speed at which any given planet will move while orbiting the sun, states that an imaginary line joining a planet to the sun will sweep out equal areas in equal times as the planet orbits the ellipse.

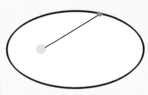

Kepler's first law of planetary motion

The third law states that the squares of the periods of the planets are proportional to the cubes of their semimajor axes. In other words, planets move in an orderly, balanced path, but each planet moves at a different speed relative to how close it is to the sun, and the changes in velocity can be calculated.

These three laws were critical to later developments, particularly the breakthroughs of Isaac Newton and Halley's mapping of comets.

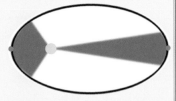

Kepler's second law of planetary motion

Access to new equipment and Flamsteed's support prompted Halley to begin focusing on the planets. The ancient Greeks believed planets moved at a steady pace around the sun, and some astronomers still believed that. But Halley ignored these old concepts and began working on a paper, using the data he accumulated through his own and Flamsteed's observations, to verify Kepler's laws of motion. It was a challenging problem, exactly the sort Halley liked. Later astronomers would have calculus to determine the changing velocities of planetary orbits, but this mathematical breakthrough had not yet come into general use. Instead, Halley used geometry to track the planets' elliptical orbits and algebraic analysis to calculate. It was not original work—he was seeking to prove Kepler's breakthroughs from early in the century. But it revealed an independence of thought and imagination and proved he was more than a gifted observer. The paper he wrote was published in 1676 and gained him even more notice.

Encouraged by his success, Halley began to work out geometrical formulas to predict where and when on the earth's surface a total eclipse of the sun would be visible. The shadow of the moon cast on Earth during an eclipse is small, covering only a few square miles at a time, and it moved quickly. Detailed calculations were needed to predict exactly where the shadow would fall at a given moment. It would help give accurate measurements of the moon as well. Flamsteed published his results several years later in the preface of his book *Doctrine of the Sphere.*

Halley was making great strides, and his professors recognized his talents as a scientist. But he decided to leave school to take advantage of an opportunity to add to the world's understanding of the heavens.

Flamsteed had made significant advances in Greenwich, producing star positions correct within ten seconds of arc. Other experts, such as Johannes Hevelius, who worked in Danzig, Poland, and J.D. Cassini in Paris were also preparing charts for a new catalog of stars north of the equator. Each used a slightly different method of observation that would have to be made uniform later. But at the time the field of star mapping was quite crowded in Europe and offered little opportunity for young Halley to earn the distinction he fervently wanted.

However, an entire half of the sky in the southern hemisphere was largely neglected. Mariners were exploring and

Halley was commissioned by the King of England to map the stars of the southern hemisphere. His tracking station was set up at St. Helena, a small island off the coast of Africa.

trading all over the world and needed astronomical charts to sail safely in the southern as well as the northern hemisphere. It was a golden opportunity for a young man with Halley's gifts and economic support to distinguish himself. Apparently, in Halley's estimation, it was worth leaving school to pursue.

Characteristically, he was not bashful about submitting his name to Flamsteed and, in turn, to the king of England, to be put in charge of a project to map the southern sky. The king, who knew how valuable the information could be to his island nation, was encouraging. The first question to be decided was where to set up Halley's tracking station. He sought advice and accepted the suggestion that the island of St. Helena would be best. St. Helena was only a dot on the map, twelve hundred miles west of Africa, positioned at a latitude of sixteen degrees south. Owned by the East India Company, the company had no problem allowing use of its land, and it even offered the young astronomer free passage on one of its ships, the *Unity*.

Halley's father agreed to continue giving Edmond the three hundred pounds' allowance he received while at Oxford. His financial support enabled Halley to buy the instruments he needed and to pay for an assistant. Edmond persuaded a friend named Clerke to serve as his assistant, and the pair sailed in November 1676. The twenty-year-old astronomer was ready to make a name for himself.

Halley had to specially design equipment that could be easily transported aboard ship. One of the heaviest of his instruments was a metal sextant, used to measure distance, in angles, between stars. The sextant had a five-and-a-half-foot radius and its arms and arc were made of brass that needed to be attached to a steel framework. Halley designed the instrument so it could be brought on board in pieces and assembled on land when they reached their destination.

Halley's quadrant measured the sun's altitude by moving a wooden arm and block until the shadow of the block coincided with the horizon slit. But when it was cloudy, there was a problem. To improve the quadrant, he fitted a lens to it instead of a wooden block, which concentrated the sun's light into a bright spot on the horizon.

Halley also took along a pendulum clock to tell time at night, and he put it together on the island. Clocks were needed to make sightings on Saint Helena at the same time sightings were being made in Greenwich. This way the two sets of figures could be compared on charts. Halley also packed several telescopes, the largest of which was the twenty-four-foot long instrument he had used at home.

Because of severe weather during the voyage and on the island, the project took more than a year. Although the ship's log has been lost, we know that the 5,600-mile journey took three months.

Halley's ambition to compete with other scientists in Europe spurred him onward. It was a tough challenge: to find the apparent position of southern stars he had to measure the angle between one star and another. Also, he had to observe some stars visible in both the northern and southern skies to connect the charts and to make his records useful to other charts.

During the first month at St. Helena, the weather was miserable with hardly a single clear night. Rain and fog hung over the mountaintop where he had set up his laboratory. At night, Halley and Clerke took naps and waited for a break in the clouds. But they slowly completed their observations.

By November of 1677, Halley sent a progress report on his star chart, as well as one on his observations of an eclipse of the sun and one of the moon. He mentioned that he had found "three Stars of the first Magnitude" that never appear in England. He also described his observation of the transit of Mercury across the face of the sun—observations he would later use in determining the distance of the sun from Earth. To honor King Charles II for his help, Halley named a new constellation *Robur Carolinum*, Latin for "Charles's Oak."

During his year on the island, Halley charted the positions of 341 stars, many of which had not been shown on a star map. After returning to London, he recorded his findings in a book written in Latin with a one-hundred-two-word title most often referred to in English as *The Catalog of the Southern Stars*. It was the first study ever made of the southern skies

Complete 102-word title of Halley's book

The English translation of the complete title of *The Catalog of the Southern Stars* is: "A catalogue of the Southern Stars, or a supplement to the Catalogue of Tycho showing the longitudes and latitudes of the Stars, which being close to the southern pole are invisible from the Uraniborg of Tycho, accurately reckoned from measured distances and completely corrected in the year 1677, with those very observations of the heavens produced with the greatest care and a sufficiently large sextant on the island of St. Helena which lies in the latitude 15 degrees 15minutes south and longitude 7 degrees, 00 minutes west of London. A labour so far needed in Astronomy, to which is added a small note covering things not unwanted in Astronomy."

King Charles II

based on actual telescopic observations, rather than sightings by the naked eye.

In the preface, Halley pointed out that the existing tables of planetary motions contained errors. For example, the commonly accepted rate of Jupiter's motion was too slow, and Saturn's too fast. To correct these errors by telescopic observation, Halley needed to redetermine the position of certain stars, because the positions of planets were understood according to their relationship with major stars in the sky.

One of Halley's most significant observations on St. Helena concerned his pendulum clock. He found that to keep time as accurately as it had in England it was necessary to shorten the pendulum. Nowadays, we know the alteration was required because the earth bulges outward at the equator. Because of the bulge, the gravitational force changes slightly around the equator. Halley's alteration of the pendulum would later be of interest to Isaac Newton.

On his return, Halley presented a copy of *The Catalog of the Southern Stars* to King Charles II, with the hope that he might receive a favor in return. The flattery worked. He was rewarded with a master of arts degree from Queen's College at Oxford without the "condition of performing any precious or subsequent exercises for the same." No final exam was required; Edmond Halley's university education was complete. Most importantly, Halley had earned a reputation as a first-rate astronomer.

three

FRIENDS
AND
ENEMIES

Halley returned to England flush with success. He accomplished what he set out to do in St. Helena and also received his Oxford degree. Still living off of his father's allowance, he did not need to find steady employment right away. He began meeting and corresponding with the other prominent scientists in England and Europe. He wanted to know about their work, if their papers were being published, and if there was anything he could do to help.

Halley had succeeded in winning over Flamsteed. Among the other prominent men of science, he wanted to meet Johannes Hevelius in Danzig, Poland. Hevelius had a 150-foot-long telescope, one of the greatest ever built, but made the strange claim that he never used telescopes on his measuring instruments. Instead he used a scope with "open sights" to map the heavens. The open sight was similar to a rifle sight, although more elaborate, and had been used by Hevelius's tutor, Peter Kruger, a respected astronomer of the earlier generation. Using open sights was generally regarded as a less accurate method of observation than using a telescope, since an open sight involved basically "eye-balling" the sky.

Galileo Galilei used a telescope to discover the phases of the orbit of Venus.

However, there had been controversy over the use of telescopes dating back to when the Italian Galileo Galilei first used one to reveal the phases of Venus in 1609. Skeptics claimed that magnified observations were not accurate because there was no way to be certain that what was seen was not actually a distortion caused by the instrument. Problems with light diffusion could distort measurements in the reflecting lens in early telescopes. One of Isaac Newton's early projects was to devise a more accurate refracting telescope to help manage the problem of light diffusion, and by 1678 most sky watchers were using telescopes. Hevelius's figures were rejected by some astronomers, which made him so angry he announced that, since no one had yet proved his figures were at fault, he would continue to use the same procedure for all future work. He claimed to have more experience than his detractors, and said that he expected an apology unless proof of inaccuracy was presented immediately.

In England, Flamsteed decided that, to settle the controversy, someone should work with Hevelius and examine how he had arrived at his published results. Halley took on the assignment, but realized it would take diplomacy. He was savvy enough to know he should not become embroiled in the argument over open sights and looked for a way to work with Hevelius while also reporting honestly on his findings. He sent him a copy of his *Catalogue of Southern Stars* as an introduction to his own work, and then added some questions that he hoped the teacher would answer. Hevelius was delighted with the gift and impressed with the young man's talent.

At Flamsteed's request, Halley sent another letter to Hevelius suggesting that perhaps he might compare Halley's figures to some of his own. The mere suggestion had to be handled with tact—after all, here was twenty-two-year-old Halley, offering to use his work to check the veracity of Hevelius's lifetime of work. Again, a certain amount of flattery cleared the way, and Hevelius eventually invited Halley to come to Danzig.

Despite the the open sight controversy, in the 1670s, Hevelius was still considered to be a master astronomer. Born in 1611 at the important port of Danzig, Poland, his father owned a flourishing brewery, which meant that, much like Halley, Hevelius was assured the best education money could buy. His tutor Peter Kruger, a gifted mathematician with an enthusiasm for astronomy, taught Hevelius the basics of planetary motion and showed him how to predict the dates of solar and lunar eclipses. Kruger also suggested that Hevelius learn drawing and the skill of engraving copper plates for book illustrations.

Hevelius also studied law, but after viewing a solar eclipse in 1639, decided to devote as much time as possible on astronomy. He set up an observatory and made all of his own instruments. He even taught himself the specialized art of grinding and polishing lenses. As mentioned, his largest telescope was 150 feet long, but he did not use it for measuring planetary or stellar positions, only for observing details such as spots on the moon and the sun.

Helvelius called astronomy a hobby, even though his observatory was considered one of the best in Europe. In 1649 his father died, leaving him with the time-consuming job of overseeing the brewery. He also became involved in the politics of the city council of Danzig. His wife was a critical helpmate who took on much of the work of managing the brewery, leaving him time to do his observations. She died in 1662

Johannes Hevelius, aided by his wife Elisabetha, used open sights to observe the heavens.

and the next year, over the age of fifty himself, he married Catherina Elisabetha, a sixteen-year-old, who immediately began helping run the brewery business and assisting her husband in his astronomical work.

Among his publications were maps of the moon's surface that he engraved, printed, and published himself, and a book on comets. After the publication of his comet book, it was announced that he used open sights on all his measuring instruments, and his figures came into question.

The day—or rather the night—that Halley arrived in Danzig, the two astronomers set to work, checking figures using their two different methods of observation. Halley stayed with Hevelius for two months, and was soon writing to Flamsteed to describe the accuracy of Hevelius's measurements. "You will find the same distance 6 times observed on Page 272 of ye fourth book of his Machina Coclestis, so that I dare no more doubt of his Veracitye."

Hevelius was delighted to have the young astronomer working with him. The friendship between Halley and Hevelius lasted until Hevelius's death in 1687, but it also created a crack in his relationship with Flamsteed, and the rift would eventually grow into an intense rivalry. Halley's testimonial also failed to convince other astronomers, particularly those in England and France, of the Polish scientist's accuracy.

Soon after Halley returned to England, Hevelius and his beautiful young wife, Elisabetha, went on vacation. While they were away, a devastating fire reduced the stable and the observatory to ashes. Flames destroyed all the books waiting to be bound, and many in the library. With Hevelius's records now gone, no one else could verify the accuracy of his figures.

It later became clear that some of Hevelius's figures were not as good as Halley had first believed. Halley also, eventually, admitted he had not been overly impressed with the 150-foot telescope. The telescope's supports were not rigid, and the instrument's sections often could not be lined up. Yet Halley preferred to maintain his relationship with Hevelius rather than publicize his shortcomings. This tact did not always please other scientists, particularly in England. Rumors even began to circulate that during Halley's visit to Poland, he and Elizabetha had had an affair. Flamsteed, a very serious-minded man, who was already disappointed that Halley had not been more vocal in his criticism of Flamsteed, believed the rumors. He publicly announced that Halley's endorsement of Hevelius's work should be doubted.

Flamsteed might just have been jealous that his former protege was beginning to outshine him. There was also the question of national pride in a competition between a Polish

Halley worked with Hevelius in Danzig, Poland, for two months.

and English astronomer. Whatever the reasons, the warm bond between Halley and Flamsteed was broken. When Hevelius died in 1687, the value of his legacy remained unresolved.

Halley did not let Flamsteed's attack knock him off his stride. He maintained his mostly even demeanor and continued his scientific pursuits. Unlike many other scientists and philosophers of the era, he generally avoided the disputes and jealous backbiting that often plagued relationships. This gift of personality increasingly pushed him into roles that required great diplomacy and tact.

After returning from Poland, Halley divided his time between Oxford and London. He lived a life of relative comfort and industriousness, attending meetings of the Royal Society. In London, he could often be found at the fashionable coffeehouses, such as Jonathan's, in Change Alley, which had become a meeting place for many members of the Royal Society, including Robert Hooke and Christopher Wren.

At the end of 1680, Halley decided to take his delayed Grand Tour of Europe. Travel would give him a chance "to converse with the astronomers and other Learned Men" of France and Italy. He was accompanied by Robert Nelson, the son of another businessman, whose father provided a generous allowance. Nelson was a devout young man who wrote poetry. The two were the same age and remained friends their entire lives.

It was on this trip that Halley saw his first comet. The comet's appearance excited all of his contemporaries. It was clearly visible from the streets of cities like London and Paris—partly because cities had no electric lighting to obscure the night sky—on clear nights.

Halley recorded his frequent sightings of the comet from the ship. He frequently wrote in Latin, as most scientists of his era did, in his notebook. It was still the universal language of the educated classes in Europe. The notes could be understood by native speakers of French, German, Italian, Norwegian, or any other language. On the notebook's cover, he wrote:

> Edmond Halley, his Booke
> And he douth often in it Looke.

Once in Paris, Halley immediately contacted Giovanni Domenico Cassini, director of the observatory. Halley's reputation preceded him, and he was invited to view the comet from this vantage point. Although he later admitted

In 1680, Giovanni Domenico Cassini was the director of the observatory in Paris.

he found Cassini's instruments inferior to those Flamsteed had at Greenwich, he was grateful for the invitation and for the use of books, which gave the most up-to-date theories about the course of comets. Interestingly, Cassini had a theory that this comet had appeared before, a theory Halley returned to later.

Tycho Brahe drew this image of the comet he observed in 1577.

Flamsteed was one of many astronomers fascinated with comets. There had actually been two sightings of comets, one in 1680, the other in 1681. Isaac Newton originally thought there were two separate comets, but in a series of letters, Flamsteed convinced him that it was actually the same comet. At the first sighting, it was moving toward the sun, Flamsteed said, and the second time it was moving away from the sun.

The central question presented by comets was the the shape of their orbits. Kepler had thought comets traveled in a straight line. Cassini thought comets traveled in circular orbits and that the comet of 1680 was the same one sighted by Tycho Brahe in 1577. The idea that comets returned was intriguing, but no observations of this or any comet's progress indicated a circular motion. The most likely shape of its path was an ellipse or a parabola.

Newton devoted a great deal of his time to trying to determine the shape of an comet's orbit. It was one of the

Ellipses and Parabolas

An ellipse, like a parabola, is an example of a curve known as a "conic section." Mathematicians have shown that a solid cone may be sliced in four different ways to produce an ellipse, a parabola, a circle, or a hyperbola. An ellipse (like a circle) is a closed figure—you may trace a pencil around an ellipse or circle and return to your starting point. A parabola, like a hyperbola, is an open curve that does not circle back on itself. Each curve is described by a different mathematical equation and each has its own unique shape.

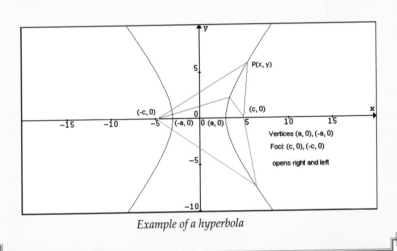

Example of a hyperbola

sections in his masterwork, *Principia*, that he worked on the longest, and one of the sections he would revise in later editions. His work on comets would have a profound influence on Halley when he turned his attention to them years later.

In Paris, Halley compiled a table of figures to compare the population density between London and Paris, and to compare death and birth rates of the two cities by checking on burial records, weddings, and christenings. Today, life insurance companies base their figures on statistics just like the ones Halley compiled; a person who specializes in such statistics is known as an actuary. Ten years later, Halley published a scientific paper on the subject. He was never one to waste time, even when traveling for pleasure.

Halley and Nelson continued on to Italy, where they toured the countryside and the great city of Rome. Halley busied himself comparing the ways the Greeks and Romans measured the foot. Nelson also made a discovery: a young widow, the daughter of the Earl of Berkeley, whom he soon married.

The Grand Tour over, Halley returned to England. Soon after his homecoming, his father remarried. Father and son

Halley and Robert Nelson visited Rome as a part of their Grand Tour. (Library of Congress)

had been close, but the new Mrs. Halley did not make her stepson feel welcome. Following the wedding, young Halley was rarely invited for visits or dinner, although the new Mrs. Halley instituted a lavish schedule of entertainment in the home.

However, romance was in the air for the son as well. Within three months, the younger Halley married Mary Tooke, the daughter of a bank official, described as "a young lady equally amiable for the gracefullness of her person and the beauties of her mind." Their wedding took place on April 20, 1682, at St. James's church in London. The young couple set up house in the nearby village of Islington, where Halley moved his astronomical equipment.

Halley and Mary had one son, whom they called Edmond after father and grandfather. They also had two daughters, Margaret and Katherine. Now ensconced in a content domestic life, Halley returned to his scientific research just in time to begin observing another comet. This comet, which appeared in late 1682 and returned in 1683, is the one that would later be given his name. Halley charted its path with the same sextant he had used to map the stars in St. Helena. After the comet left, Halley put away his data and turned to other projects.

four

THE ROYAL SOCIETY

On the morning of March 5, 1684, Edmond Halley Sr. told his wife he would be back by evening, and went on a walk. Before leaving, he complained his shoes felt tight and pinched his feet. One of his nephews, who was visiting at the time, suggested that he remove the lining in his shoes to make them more comfortable. After following his nephew's advice, Halley Sr. left the house. When his body was found in a river a week later, his clothes had been stripped. The nephew was able to identify the corpse by its stockings and shoes. Apparently the dead man's face was unrecognizable, disfigured by days spent in the water.

How the elder Halley died remains a mystery. One theory

was that he might have committed suicide, because his second marriage was unhappy. Halley's wife tended toward extravagance, and the couple was rumored to have financial difficulties. However, a jury decided that Halley's father had been murdered and robbed. To make matters worse, he left no will, and Halley and his stepmother argued over how to divide the estate. Their struggle eventually led to a lawsuit.

While there is no evidence that Halley was destitute, the loss of his father's financial backing made it necessary for him to find gainful employment. Luckily, the Royal Society, which he belonged to, was looking to hire a clerk.

The Royal Society of London for the Improvement of Natural Knowledge was incorporated in 1663.

The Royal Society of London for the Improvement of Natural Knowledge had been formally incorporated in 1663. It was the first-ever, state-sponsored organization dedicated to the promotion of science. The Royal Society's roots stretched back to an informal group of what was called Natural Philosophers, which met at Gresham College in London. The group included the chemist Robert Boyle, who first hired a young Robert Hooke as an assistant, and Christopher Wren. During this series of informal meetings, a group of seven professors gave lectures on astronomy, divinity, geometry, law, medicine, music, and rhetoric.

Robert Boyle

Christopher Wren

During the civil war, some of the scientists had moved to Oxford, and meetings began to be held there, too. When the political climate stabilized, Charles II gave the informal group, many of whom had supported the royalist side during the long conflict, a Royal Charter.

By 1685, the Royal Society's work had increased to such a level that the honorary, unpaid secretaries could no longer handle the tasks of answering correspondence, arranging and reporting on meetings, and publishing the journal *Philosophical*

Transactions. They decided to employ a paid officer to act as clerk and assist the secretaries.

A number of Fellows of the Society applied for the post. Edmond Halley received the greatest number of votes, but one rule had to be changed to allow him to take the job. The chosen candidate was supposed to be a single man living at Gresham College, and Halley was married. The original Charter of the Society also stated that Fellows could have their out-of-pocket expenses paid, but they could not receive a salary. The Society would not alter this rule. Because Halley could not remain a Fellow and receive a salary, he resigned his membership in the Society, a post he had cherished since his twenty-second birthday, in 1678. It may have seemed like a demotion, but Halley was happy to have the job. He needed the income, and it put him at the center of everything that went on in the Royal Society. As it turned out, his scientific knowledge was enhanced by the clerking job, and his acquaintances among other scientists multiplied.

The results of all new scientific research projects conducted between 1685 and 1696 passed across Halley's desk. He replied

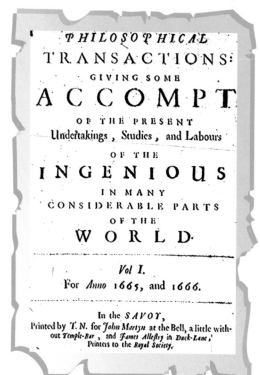

The cover of the first edition of Philosophical Transactions.

to scores of scientific questions and sent out many letters asking for information to further his own work. It demanded that he learn about scientific subjects far outside his areas of expertise. People often sent him strange rocks and petrified animals for identification, for example, and he diligently tried to help them out. He worked to answer every request, either through research of his own or by referring questions to others more qualified on the subject.

One of the letters that crossed Halley's desk was from a Mr. Francis Davenport, who had made note of the irregular tides along the coast of southeastern China. The figures seemed to become more inconsistent at definite seasons of the year, particularly during the monsoons. Initially, Davenport thought the geography of the shoreline might have an effect, but he also speculated, along with others, that the gravitational force of the moon might control the tides. Halley took up the challenge of investigating this hypothesis.

After observing the tides, Halley made graphs to show that the increase in tides corresponded with "the position of the moon with respect to those points in the sky where the sun's path and the celestial equator cross." This was fairly easy to do, but the graphs did not explain why there was a relationship between the moon and the tides. That explanation would come later.

Halley also edited the *Philosophical Transactions,* the most important English scientific journal of the day. As clerk and editor, he frequently settled arguments between scientists, a jealous lot that often quarreled over the question of who had discovered what first.

During this era, when interest in science was high and many people were pursuing new avenues, more than one person would sometimes make the same discovery at nearly the same time. These disputes over priority, which often grew very heated, Halley handled with patience. He listened to both sides of an argument and frequently helped the two parties reach a compromise. It was his job to give credit where it was due, but that was often difficult to determine. His most common suggestion was to add the names of several claimants to the published papers and to convince them to share credit. He was also responsible for communicating new discoveries, which helped to establish priority. He would copy data and have it sent via ship or carriage to other countries or areas in England in order to make others aware of new discoveries. Sometimes this could take the better part of a year.

There were many instances where Halley actually gave other scientists credit when he could prove he had thought of something first. For example, Jacob Bernouilli published a paper involving values of conic sections, which was very similar to a paper Halley had previously authored. Because Bernouilli published first, the honor of discovery went to him, although Halley's figures were on file with the Royal Society. Halley never contested Bernouilli's claim.

The clerk job kept Halley busy attending meetings, taking minutes, and dealing with the correspondence. He also found time to continue his own research. During 1686 and 1687 he produced a large number of papers. In one project, he tracked the moon as it passed in front of Jupiter in order to measure the moon's exact position.

Halley turned his attention from the sky to study how the figures on a barometer changed, depending on its height above sea level and changes in weather. He climbed the mountains himself to conduct the experiments, seldom using an assistant.

The facts he presented were helpful, but it was hard to pinpoint the reason for changes in barometric pressure.

A more important paper was titled "An Historical Account of the Trade winds and monsoons, observable in the seas near the tropics, with an attempt to assign the physical cause of the winds." Trade winds always blow in the same direction at the same time of the year. Halley noted that the trade winds are limited to a band of some thirty degrees of latitude around the earth, both below and above the equator. He wanted to know what caused this continuous blast of air. (Today, we know that winds are caused by the sun heating the atmosphere. The sun's radiation hits the earth most directly at the equator. The warm air rises and cooler air streams in to replace it. The existence of large bodies of land, and the earth's rotation, also affects wind direction.)

Devising a mathematical formula to explain the patterns of the trade winds was a difficult challenge. Halley was not able to answer all the questions about trade winds, but did devise a method for meteorological charting that is still used by cartographers. He showed the winds on his map by short dotted lines, connecting the points where the variation was the same, while each elongated dot had a thick front and a thin tail to show the direction of the wind.

Another paper he wrote during this time was a practical discussion of how to aim heavy artillery shells. Factoring in gravitational force, he worked out a formula of how to adjust the elevation of a large gun by using a stationary metal plate and a plumb line. His figures increased accuracy tenfold.

One of his unpublished papers dated March 6, 1689, was entitled "A Method of Walking under Water." In it, he proposed a practical means of collecting treasure from shipwrecks.

The shape of the diving bell allowed air to be trapped at the top. (Courtesy of Henrik Reinholdson)

Because this offered the possibility of great rewards if his theories proved practical, investors came forward to finance the equipment. Halley's sketches called for a hollow, spherical- or cylindrical-shaped copper or wooden tub, open at the bottom with a height twice as great as the diameter. To make the vessel, which he called a diving bell, heavy enough to sink, he specified brass or lead wheels so it could be shoved along the sea bed. Barrels of compressed air would be sent down and pumped into the diving bell. Halley estimated that at a depth of thirty feet, the air would take over half the volume of the tub; at one hundred feet it would take up only a quarter of the space. By continually pumping in more air to take up room inside the sphere, he figured the water could be kept below a diver's knees. The diver would wear boots like a fishermen and could stay clothed and dry even "'tho it be 20 fathoms deep." Halley's design provided a window at the top and a valve to let out the "hott and effete air unfit for further respiration."

The Royal Society persuaded the Admiralty to use one of the Navy's frigates to take the apparatus out to a shallow bed of the sea. To prove his confidence in this new form of habitat, Halley volunteered to make the original dive. It was not a pleasant adventure. He wrote:

> When we lett down this engine into the sea we all found at first a forceable and painful pressure on our Ears which grew worse and worse till something in the ear gave way to the Air to enter, which gave present ease, and at length we found that Oyle of Sweet Almonds in the Ears, facilitated much this admittance of the Air and took of the aforesaid pain almost wholly.

The air supply was lowered in iron-bound, lead-covered casks from the boat on the surface. Each forty-gallon cask had a stoppered hole in the bottom and a valve in the top. When lowered under and into the diving bell, the air in the cask was released, driving out the water in the diving bell. Every fifteen feet, they repeated the procedure. It was cumbersome, but it worked. Halley survived, attesting to the success of his invention. He bragged in his report to the Society that "I have kept 3 men 1 ¾ [hours] under the water in ten fathoms deep without any the least inconvenience and in as perfect freedom to act as if they had been above." He went on to predict that much larger diving machinery could be built for commercial purposes.

It was extremely cold working inside the diving bell. Halley tried to increase the comfort factor by designing a helmet and a leather suit that was "well liquored [oiled] . . . and close to the body." He fit a lead belt around the suit to make it easier to stay underwater.

Halley also devised a primitive type of depth gauge and invented a waterproof lantern so "I can unlade a shipp at the bottom of the sea without breaking her . . ." To utilize his inventions, he formed a public company for salvaging wrecks, which brought him monetary success for a while. Halley was not the first to design diving gear. French physicist Denis Papin had put ideas on paper, but he had not tried them out in the water. Halley, as always, wanted to be the one to test his ideas so improvements could be made.

As a secondary experiment, Halley took note of how colors changed under water. The light coming in from under the diving bell was pale green and what he saw from the window at the top of the bell was a pale cherry red. When he accidentally cut his finger, the blood looked deep green and seemed to flow more rapidly than on the surface. These observations were later incorporated in further experiments.

Halley was sometimes criticized for flitting from one subject to another, but he enriched the scientific world with his varied interests and conclusions. His theories were always bold, but he tested them when possible and based his conclusions only on his observations and measurements.

Practical questions made a big demand on Halley's time at the Society. He wrote that during the great frost of 1689 he watered herb crops with soap suds that enabled them to "bear the hard winter well." That year, he also wrote about refining silver and asserted that the best gilt wire would be made from gold film "1/345,560 part of an inch." He asked why, when homes were blown up with gunpowder—which happened during the Great Fire of London in 1666—the windows of houses nearby always fell outward into the street, not inward, and decided that sudden changes in air pressure were probably the cause.

"An Account of the Watery Vapours of the Sea, and of the cause of springs," was another topic he analyzed to develop a theory on evaporation and subsequent rainfall. These simple phenomena had not been given such serious consideration before.

Halley did not limit himself to scientific questions. He had an interest in history and the question of how to date specific events. He wanted to know the date and place Julius Caesar first landed on the British Isles. It meant translating past historians' records, logically finding where they might be wrong, and then digging in other directions to find the foundations of Roman forts that had been covered and lost. He also wrote papers on how high bullets could be shot and how fountains operated. There seemed to be no end to his imagination and his skill at unearthing proof.

Working on so many different experiments sharpened his talents as an experimenter and at thinking through problems. In 1692, a member of the Royal Society, John Houghton, asked Halley if he could measure the size of England and Wales. Houghton was studying the productivity of agricultural crops, but he had no figures on the land area. The task was challenging because the coastline of England swerves and wiggles in a very irregular pattern. Houghton wondered if Halley would have to hire a score of surveyors to map the country, county by county. Would the Royal Society agree

Seventeenth Century England

Using geometry and the largest complete map of England at the time, Halley was able to figure out the acreage of England and Wales in less than a week.

to the cost? How many years before a final figure could be presented?

Within a week, Halley handed his colleague a paper with the grand total. Houghton thought Halley was playing some kind of joke, but when asked how he had accomplished the task, the answer was simple.

Halley had taken the largest complete map of England and Wales he could find and very carefully cut the land outline from the water area. Then he weighed the paper. Next he cut out a circle from the map with exactly two degrees on the prime meridian, the imaginary north-south line on the globe that passes through Greenwich, England. Halley knew that two degrees of the meridian equaled 138 2/3 miles. Now he could figure the area of his circle in square miles, using geometry. Since the circle was only a quarter of the weight of the whole land area of England, his answer of total acreage was 38,660,000. He arrived at the final answer by weighing the circle and comparing its weight to that of the large cutout. Surprisingly, his answer was off by only 3 percent, and that deviation could be attributed to erosion.

Although still a young man, Halley was quickly emerging as one of the most brilliant experimenters in Europe. His mathematical skills and original thinking placed him in the top ranks. Soon, however, he would have to draw on his talent for diplomacy, as well as his wisdom and generosity, to succeed in his next challenge.

five

NEWTON
AND
BEYOND

Halley's eleven years as clerk of the Royal Society were busy and productive. He pursued a variety of experiments, but one puzzle took precedent over everything else. He and many of the other members of the Society wanted to determine the accuracy of Johannes Kepler's theories of planetary motion. Proving once and for all that the planets moved as Kepler had stated would answer many questions regarding the effect of gravity on moving bodies, some of which could be used to better understand comets.

In his third law, Kepler said that the time a planet takes to travel around the sun, and its average distance from the sun, are in the mathematical proportion of 2:3. After some calculation, Halley had theorized that this was because the sun

This is believed to be a portrait of Robert Hooke. (Courtesy of the Granger Collection)

attracted each planet with a force dependent on the inverse square of the distance between the sun and the planet. In other words, the sun's gravitational force diminished by four times if the distance were doubled, nine times if the distance were tripled, and so on. However, he had not been able to mathematically prove his premise.

Naturally, Halley discussed the problem with other Fellows of the Society. It was one of the most intriguing and pressing problems of the time. Anyone who could produce mathematical proof of what came to be called the inverse square law would become the most famous scientist alive.

Others claimed to have made even more progress than Halley in solving the problem. Robert Hooke bragged that he had worked out a proof. Hooke was an experimentalist

Members of The Royal Society would often meet in coffeehouses.

who, much like Halley, had let his curiosity take him in many directions. However, he developed a habit of making claims he could not substantiate. He was also different than Halley in that he had a reputation for being argumentative and jealous of other's success. Earlier, in 1672, he had engaged in a controversy with Isaac Newton over the properties of light. Newton was so offended that he retreated to his rooms in Cambridge, swore off participating in Royal Society activities, and pursued his research in private.

Halley and others urged Hooke to share his proof, but it was not forthcoming. Then, one day at the coffeehouse in January 1684, Christopher Wren set up a contest. Whoever could come up with the proof first would win the prize of a book of their own choice, but not to exceed the value of two pounds.

Halley was spurred onward by the challenge, not for the sake of winning a book, but for the prestige in solving the problem. Yet, he was still unable to crack the problem, and Hooke was not forthcoming with an answer. However, he had heard that Newton might have the proof of this inverse square law.

Rumors and unsubstantiated stories about the work Newton was doing had circulated for years. However, Newton seldom ventured far from Trinity College in Cambridge, especially after his dispute with Hooke. One of the rumors was that he had come up with a proof of the inverse square law. No one knew for certain if it was true, but the little of his work made public convinced Halley and others that if anyone had accomplished it, Newton had.

Halley traveled to Cambridge to see if he could entice Newton out of his isolation. After a bumpy fifty-mile trip by stagecoach, Halley reached the great man for the first time. Newton was notoriously difficult to talk with, much less get close to, but the two men quickly warmed to each other. Halley was respectful and enthusiastic and, most importantly, willing to pay homage to Newton, who was fourteen years older. Soon they were deep into a scientific conversation, and Halley asked Newton what would be the shape of the orbit of the planets if the inverse square law was true. An ellipse, Newton immediately responded. Furthermore, he had worked it out mathematically years before and had the proof somewhere.

Halley was stunned that Newton had not shared this knowledge with his fellow scientists. He might also have been a little skeptical. After all, Hooke had been making the same claim but had yet to produce it. Halley asked to see the proof, but Newton could not find it. Halley urged him to recompose it and send it to him for publication. He also agreed to help Newton avoid the type of controversy he had been forced to deal with before. This would later turn out to be a challenge when Hooke inevitably claimed he had done it first. Newton, impressed with Halley's sincerity and aware of his reputation for fairness and honesty, promised to work it all out again and send it to Halley as soon as possible.

It is possible Newton was growing tired of his isolation. He had made promises to others but then allowed himself to be diverted by other work. He also was no doubt aware that

Isaac Newton

the race to prove the inverse square law was on, and there was a chance someone else could beat him. Whatever the cause, Halley's visit sparked him to begin to re-engage with the Royal Society.

In November of 1684, Newton sent Halley a paper in Latin entitled "De Motu" ("On Motion"), which had the promised mathematical demonstration of how the inverse square law explained elliptical orbits. Halley realized instantly that the paper was the breakthrough he had wanted. Unlike many of his fellow researchers, Halley was not jealous of another's work. He seemed to have instantly recognized that in Newton he had found a man much more brilliant than himself and set out working to make sure his work received the audience and respect it deserved.

Nicholas Copernicus

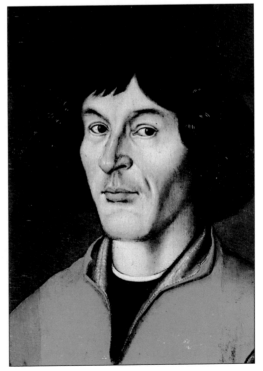

Halley began making more frequent trips to Cambridge, where he and Newton talked at great length about the mathematical proof. Some of the questions were about the entirely new type of math Newton had developed to make it easier to deal with bodies in motion that Newton called "Fluxions." Today, we call it calculus.

Newton was still hesitant to publish. He dreaded the criticism he was sure his unusual conclusions would bring. But Halley would not be put off. He pushed Newton to develop his theories of motion, which promised once and for all to demonstrate that the same physical properties that operated on Earth, many of which had first been laid out by Galileo earlier in the century, also held sway over the heavens. Halley realized that Newton's work was on the verge of synthesizing the last 150 years of advancements in physics and astronomy—the work of Copernicus, Kepler, and Galileo—into a single system. But it would take more than a single paper. As an added encouragement to Newton, Halley urged the Royal Society to pay for the publication of Newton's work, but the funds were not available. Undeterred, Halley decided to pay for the printing out of his own pocket, and he even put aside his own work for a year and a half to help organize and proof the material. This was a remarkable act of generosity.

As expected, Robert Hooke began to claim that he had already developed some of the ideas in "On Motion." When Newton heard of Hooke's claims he threatened to destroy the last section of the report, but Halley had anticipated this would happen and was able to soothe his feelings. He also pressured other members of the Society, particularly Christopher Wren, to convince Hooke to back off his claim.

Encouraged by Halley, Newton engaged in one of the most productive periods of his life. Soon after he began writing, both Newton and Halley realized it would take more than a single volume. In the end, the actual work was divided into three sections. Newton waited until the final section to lay out his analysis of the orbits of comets, the motion of the

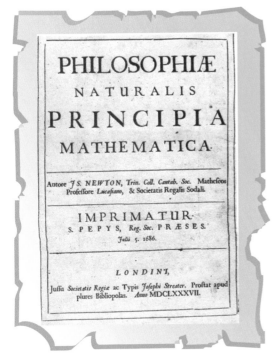

PHILOSOPHIÆ
NATURALIS
PRINCIPIA
MATHEMATICA

Autore J S. NEWTON, Trin. Coll. Cantab. Soc. Matheseos
Professore Lucasiano, & Societatis Regalis Sodali.

IMPRIMATUR
S. PEPYS, Reg. Soc. PRÆSES.
Julii 5. 1686.

LONDINI,
Jussu Societatis Regiæ ac Typis Josephi Streater. Prostat apud
plures Bibliopolas. Anno MDCLXXXVII.

With Halley's encouragement and help, Newton published Mathematical Principles of Natural Philosophy.

planets, and the relationship between relative masses and gravitational attraction exerted by the sun and planets, all questions that had never been solved.

Newton's masterwork was published in 1687, titled *Mathematical Principles of Natural Philosophy*, and is most commonly referred to as the *Principia*. Halley paid for the entire first publication of the three volumes. In the *Principia* Newton explained that the force—which he called gravity—that makes an apple fall to the ground is also the force that keeps the moon in its orbit around the earth, and keeps all the planets moving on paths around the sun. For the first time, someone was able to verify that Kepler's laws were right—and to explain why they were right. He also laid out his own laws of force and mass, inertia, and motion in concise formulas.

Albert Einstein

Newton's massive work stood unchallenged until the twentieth century, when Albert Einstein's theories of relativity and the discoveries in quantum physics forced a rethinking of how nature works at the extremes of size and speed.

Newton paid tribute to Halley's assistance in the preface: "In publication of this work the most astute and universally learned Mr. Edmund Halley not only assisted me in correcting errors of the press and preparing the geometrical figures, but it was through his solicitations that it came to be published . . ."

Halley provided his own review of the work. "It may be justly said, that so many and so Valuable Philosophical Truths, as are herein discovered, and put past Dispute, were never yet owing to the Capacity and Industry of Man." After the publication of *Principia,* Isaac Newton was hailed as the greatest scientist of his, and quite possibly any, time, but without Edmond Halley, the world might never have learned of Newton's work.

Halley did benefit from his association with Newton. Newton's calculus would later give him a critical tool to map comets. Halley had come to agree with Cassini that comets returned and that the one from 1692 he had been able to observe the longest, would return. But there were still few who agreed with him, and he still could not prove it. Compared to understanding the orbits of comets, planets were easy. Even Newton admitted that he did not yet thoroughly understand how they traveled. But the new method of measuring the dynamics of a body in motion, at varying speeds, might help to map out a schedule for the comet's return. It would take Halley until 1705 before he had finished his figures and felt confident enough to publish them.

The circumstances of Halley's life were another hindrance to his work on the comet. During this time, while Halley was busy with Newton's *Principia*, the Royal Society could not afford to pay him. Part of the Society's financial problems can be attributed to political turmoil in England. Following the death of Charles II, James II was crowned king in 1685. James was a Roman Catholic, and to the consternation of many, he began to fill important vacancies in the government with men of his own faith. Some people feared that England would soon return to Catholicism, others dreaded the more likely prospect of another period of religious violence. In France, the French king Louis XIV had already revoked the Edict of

King James II

After the Glorious Revolution, King James II was forced to give up the throne of England. His daughter Mary and William of Orange were named joint monarchs by Parliament in 1689.

Nantes that had granted freedom of worship to the French Protestants. Soon the Protestants, called Huguenots, began showing up in England seeking sanctuary. Many members of the Royal Society in England slipped out of London to avoid getting caught up in the conflict. This led to a drop in funding and a withdrawing of support for scientific studies already in the works. It was costly to keep the clerk's office open and to print the backlog of reports that detailed the scientific work being carried on, and Halley was soon out of a job.

After only a three-year reign, James was finally forced to give up the throne in a nearly bloodless revolt sometimes called the Glorious Revolution. A group of members of Parliament and prominent Protestants secretly agreed to support William of Orange, husband of James' estranged Protestant daughter Mary, if he agreed to invade England to overthrow the king. William and Mary would then reside as joint monarchs. When William and his force, which clearly overwhelmed anything James could hope to raise, landed in the north of England in November of 1688 the king fled to France. William and Mary were proclaimed joint monarchs in 1689.

The succession crisis created controversy and deep unease in the country. Few wanted a repeat of the strife that had been so destructive only a few decades before. Halley, always the negotiator, tried to keep an impartial attitude. He is reported as saying: "For my part, I am for the King in possession. If I am protected, I am content. I am sure we pay dear enough for our Protection & why should we not have the Benefit of it?"

However, even Halley could not straddle the gulf that existed between Catholics and Protestants. He openly rejected the idea that a comet had caused the biblical flood that Noah survived, which offended many. He also alienated both branches of the church with his controversial ideas of the age of the earth. Those who calculated time by strictly counting "begats"—the number of generations listed in the Bible from Adam to Jesus—came up with the date of creation as 4004 B.C. One college chancellor even declared that Adam was created at nine o'clock in the morning on Sunday, October 23, 4004 B.C.

Halley was sure that the earth was much older and wanted to find scientific proof. He tried to estimate the earth's age by measuring the saltiness of the oceans, but this was not practical. He did note that seashells could be found high above the present ocean level—in one case on a mountain slope. So how could such a huge landmass upheaval have occurred without some civilization having recorded it? To many people outside of the scientific world, this was blasphemy and his reputation was damaged.

However, the government soon needed his help. King William had become worried about the devaluation of English currency. In those days, money existed in coins, not in paper bills, and the value of the silver in the coins was supposed to match the face value. But the coins had smooth edges, which made it easy for criminals to gouge pieces of silver from the edge and melt it down. People often did not notice the nicks in the coins, and the scarred currency went back into circulation. Over time, however, because the coins had been clipped, English money was losing its value.

The king tried to get a law passed to assess the value of coins by weight alone, but it was an unpopular idea because thousands of coins in circulation would suddenly be worth less. Parliament did not pass the law, and in this semidemocratic political era, the king did not get his way. The only solution was to recall all scarred coins. They were to be melted down and replaced by new currency with milled, or ribbed, edges, which would make it easier to detect clipping.

This would be a massive undertaking wrought with opportunities for corruption. During the period of exchange, it would be easy to buy up the coinage at a lower rate than King William had decreed and charge the royal treasury a substantially larger amount and profit. The person chosen to oversee the currency transition must be of faultless honesty, someone who could be trusted with grave responsibilities.

Isaac Newton was the first person appointed to head the project, and he again called on his friend Halley for help. From 1696 to 1698, Edmond Halley served as deputy comptroller of the royal mint at Chester, one of five places where the new coinage was being manufactured. Though Halley was apparently not forced to give up his position of clerk to the Royal Society while he oversaw the mint, he did have to move his office and daily residence to Chester, some 175 miles northwest of London. Not usually one to complain, Halley found the job of managing the mint tedious and very different from the creative scientific work in his laboratory.

To make matters worse, he had to put up with bickering and dishonesty among the employees he had to oversee. Both Halley and the warden of the mint, a Mister Weddell, took their jobs very seriously, but the Master of the Mint, a fellow named Clark, was a braggart who rarely spent time going over figures. Clark was supposed to supervise the making of the coinage, but he usually ignored his work, and although Clark claimed to be the chief officer in charge at the mint, Halley actually had been given the superior job.

Halley and Weddell determined that two clerks at the mint, Bowles and Lewis, were skimming. However, Clark took the side of the two accused clerks. Lewis, a real troublemaker who had once thrown an ink well at Weddell, claimed that Halley and Weddell had shown favoritism in deciding who could purchase chipped coins. In other words, he accused Halley and Weddell of the crimes he himself had committed.

At one point, Halley even had to intervene to stop a duel between Bowles and Lewis. It was no wonder that Halley wanted no more part of the feuding. He finally wrote to Newton: "I guess wee shall have finished our whole coinage, which will be very near 300000 li [pounds] . . . I long to be delivered from the uneasiness I suffer here by ill company in my business, which at least is but drudgery, but as we are in perpetuall feuds it is intollerable."

Halley tried to resign his job, even though he feared that blame for the bickering at Chester might fall on him. When no replacement was assigned, he kept to his job until the work was completed.

Peter the Great

Halley was soon given another assignment by the king. Czar Peter of Russia came to England to study the more advanced science that had not yet reached his country. His primary goal was to study English shipbuilding. The famous shipyards owned by the East India Company at Deptford, England gave the czar a chance to see the latest English designs for ships that could sail regular long-distance trading routes. He was also interested in meeting some of England's brightest scientists.

While in England, Peter the Great stayed at a large country home in the town of Deptford.

Because of Halley's brilliant mind and engaging personality, he made a fine ambassador for his country. Czar Peter and his royal entourage were provided quarters in Deptford at a large country house, where Peter had a riotous time having himself wheeled around the grounds of the estate in a wheelbarrow, in the process ruining some cherished beautiful holly hedges. Halley, although never accused of such undignified behavior, frequently dined with the czar and found Peter "intelligent and amusing."

King William took note of the good feelings between the two men and kept Halley in mind when he again needed to an ambassador to other lands. The next time, though, the journey would have a scientific purpose.

six

CAPTAIN HALLEY

In 1698, after Halley had left his job at the mint in Chester and he and his family had settled back in London, King William gave him another project, one more to Halley's liking. He would lead an expedition to further investigate fluctuations in compass readings.

The idea for the expedition had been proposed by Benjamin Middleton, a newly elected member of the Royal Society. Middleton promised that if the Admiralty would build and provision him with a small vessel of about sixty tons, he planned to sail around the world to make observations on the "Magneticall Needle." Middleton soon dropped out of the picture, however, because the trip would keep him away from home too long.

Halley was the obvious choice to head such an expedition. He had continued to record compass readings ever since his stay on St. Helena. It would give him another opportunity to gather information he could use to solve some of the problems of equating longitude.

Halley was chosen by the Royal Navy to lead an expedition to explore variances in compass reading.

Despite Halley's lack of naval training, the Navy commissioned him as captain of the ship it provided for the expedition and put him in charge of the project. His orders were:

> Instructions for proceeding to Improve the knowledge of the Longitude and Variations of the Compasse. . . . You are to make the best of your way to the Southward of the Equator, and there to observe on the East Coast of South America, and the West Coast of Africa, the variations of the Compasse, with all the accuracy you can, as also the true Scitutation both in Longitude and Latitude of the Ports where you arrive.

He was further advised to visit islands "without too much deviation," and if the season of the year permitted, to sail along the coast of what we now call Australia and map the coast in detail. On the way home he was to visit the English West Indian Plantations:

> . . .or as many of them as conveniently you may, and in them to make such observations as may contribute to lay them downe truely in their Geographical Scituation. And in all the Course of your Voyage, you must be carefull not to omit no opportunity of Noteing the variation of the Compasse, of which you are to keep a Record in your Journall.

It was a tall order for even the most experienced seaman, and Halley was a landsman who spent most of his time exploring the sky.

The ship at his command, named the *Paramore,* was fifty-two feet long, eighteen feet wide, and only seven feet deep. It had a somewhat flat bottom—a design developed by the Dutch—which allowed it to sail in shallow waters. The sides of the ship bulged outward just above the waterline, providing more space for supplies. The ship's design was very unusual; it belonged to a class of vessels the Dutch called *pincke,* or *pink.* The Admiralty only owned two such ships.

Halley requested the services of a naval surgeon and a chief mate, and a crew of ten foremast men, two cabin boys, and a boatswain, gunner, and carpenter. The men were selected by the Navy, and would be paid by the king. But Halley was asked to sign a guarantee for the wages if anything went wrong.

The *Paramore* set sail October 20, 1698, and almost immediately ran into bad weather. Halley reported in the log that the ship had many defects. It leaked, and the bilge pumps continued to bring up the sand that had been loaded into the hold to give the ship extra ballast. The ship returned to port, where some of the problems were corrected, and they set out again as soon as possible to take advantage of the best possible weather in the southern hemisphere.

Pirates were known to lurk in the waters Halley was navigating, and his log reports one incident in which the *Paramore* was fired upon by two British merchant ships that mistook the unusual, flat-bottomed ship for a pirate vessel. Wherever Halley put to port, he meticulously charted the coastal area and noted the magnetic variation of compass readings. Off the coast of Brazil they took on supplies, water, tobacco, sugar, and whatever fresh produce was available. On shore he set up his long telescope and observed the end of a lunar eclipse, but complained he was unable to observe an eclipse of one of Jupiter's satellites because of bad weather.

Difficulties began to mount. Lieutenant Harrison, the second in command, refused to follow orders, assuring the crew that he, not Halley, had the training to get them home safely. In Halley's own words, "On the fifth of this month he was pleased so grosly to afront me, as to tell me before my Officers and Seamen on Deck . . . that I was not only uncapable to take charge of the Pink, but even of a Longboat."

Mutiny was averted when Halley took over complete control of the ship. He confined the lieutenant to his quarters and ordered double watches to see that his commands were followed. Once the ship returned to home port, Harrison was court-martialed. Harrison's accusations about Halley were clearly unfounded. The fact that Halley safely navigated the ship back to England from the south seas without loss of life or property showed that this mathematician, accustomed to training his sights skyward, was efficient at sea.

Upon their return, Halley planned a second voyage to continue research on charting longitude as well as latitude in the unmapped portion of the Atlantic Ocean. He was soon back at sea. During the voyage, on December 4, 1698, there was an osculation of a specific star by the moon, meaning that the moon had passed in front of the star, hiding it from view. With Halley's wonderful memory of the placement of stars in the sky, he made accurate measurements and set the exact latitude of their course. Seamen generally would not have had the skill or knowledge to accomplish this task.

By this time they were sailing due south. On February 1, 1699, the crew saw three islands straight ahead that did not appear on the charts. Halley described them as "being all flatt on the Top, and covered with snow, milk white with perpendicular cliffs. . . . The great hight of them made us conclude them land, but there was no appearance of any tree or green thing on them."

What they saw were actually huge icebergs, which could pose grave danger to the ship. Then, to make their course more dangerous, they were engulfed in a blanket of fog. Halley ordered the sails lowered, and sent a sailor out in a dingy to row a few feet ahead and give them signals to guide their passage. Luckily, they avoided a potentially disastrous end to their voyage.

They sailed north and west toward the Brazilian island of Trinidad, which Halley called Troindada. During a five-day layover they mapped the area. As usual, Halley did not take it easy. Everything he observed, from types of vegetation to animal behavior, was fodder for his journals.

It had been seven months since they set sail. Now, when they landed in the Brazilian province of Pernambuco, they were greeted with an armed guard. The Portuguese governor of Recife was following the orders of a Mr. Harwicke, who called himself an English Consul. On May 2, the *Paramore* was searched and Halley arrested. Halley brought forth his credentials as proof they were on a scientific mission. Eventually his word was believed, but not without some frightening moments.

Onward they sailed, only to be plagued again when Halley and many of his crew became sick. There was no description of their malady, but Halley remarks that he was so weak he had to take to his cabin for a week. They reached Bermuda on June 20, where the ship was put in dry dock to caulk the leaking timbers of the *Paramore*. Again, the log gives detailed figures of tides and compass readings.

They set sail from Bermuda for Cape Cod in New England, but because of bad weather continued on to Newfoundland. By the end of August, the *Paramore* had landed at Plymouth

Current map of Pernambuco, Brazil, where Halley was arrested.

Sound back in England. It was now time for Halley to record his work and present it to the king, who had sponsored both trips. The results of Halley's research were published on a map of both the North and South Atlantic. He adopted an effective means of showing the magnetic variation by using dotted lines connecting points with similar figures. These became known as *Halleyan* lines, which helped to lay the foundation of modern physical geography.

Halley's Chart of Magnetic Variation (Courtesy of the Natural Resources, Canada, Geological Survey of Canada)

The device Halley used to tell the distance traveled had been described in letters to the Royal Society in 1692. His idea was that the speed of a ship could be shown to be in proportion to the tilt from vertical of a heavy instrument towed from the stern of a ship. He worked out the figures and design for the shape of an instrument that could be towed. When towed, the device would clearly demonstrate the tilt it was undergoing and, in turn, how fast the ship was sailing.

Accuracy of Latitude and Longitude

Halley carried out most of his longitude determinations at sea by both dead reckoning and by assessing how far he had traveled. He also made observations of the moon's position with respect to nearby bright stars because, when sufficiently accurate tables of the moon became available, he believed this to be the most practical method.

Halley used a sextant on board. His tabulated values of longitude were only given to the nearest minute of the arc's degree, which was not accurate enough to solve the longitude problem. He also observed occultations of stars—timing the exact moment one star passed by another, blocking its sight from the observer. It was more accurate, but still not close enough.

On shore it was easier to determine longitude. Halley set up his telescope and a pendulum clock and made his calculations based on observations of Jupiter's satellites. Comparing these figures with known satellite positions at Greenwich time, his computations came within the required accuracy of some thirty to sixty miles.

Latitude was a much simpler matter. Sextant measurements of the altitude of the sun by day and the Pole Star or other stars at night brought about accuracy to within twenty miles or so.

After his return to London, it would have been natural to take a break, but Halley's reputation opened other avenues of research. Once more he had to take leave of his family. Again he would be sailing the *Paramore*, but this time much closer to home.

Halley was commissioned to determine the tides along the coasts of the British Channel, on both the English and the French coast. He mapped both good landing harbors and inhospitably steep promontories.

This job was undertaken just before the War of Spanish Succession in 1702, when tensions were high, and the always tense English-French diplomatic ties were strained to the breaking point. Halley's orders may even have included a darker purpose—spying on the enemy. Whether Halley knew it or not, the information he collected was invaluable to the British Navy, who sided with Spain during the war.

Halley fulfilled two more diplomatic errands as captain of a ship in 1702 and 1703. Queen Anne sent him to Vienna at the request of Emperor Leopold of Austria, who had signed treaties with the English and Dutch. Halley was to go as technical adviser to counsel the emperor on fortifications of harbors in Istria on the Balkan coast. The emperor was impressed with the scientific knowledge Halley shared with him, and presented Halley with a diamond ring.

Halley returned to Austria once more to see how the work was progressing. Both trips involved extensive travel and might have been used as a cover for spying. He returned to England in November 1703 with a letter dated January 14, 1704, from the Earl of Nottingham, instructing the Chancellor of the Exchequer to pay Halley a sum of thirty-six pounds for Halley's expenses "out of the secret service."

Halley hoped to get an academic post. Twelve years earlier, he had applied for the position of Savilian Chair of Astronomy at Oxford, but a man named John Wallis received the job instead. Wallis had recently died, and Halley was the logical person to succeed him. But his old enemy Flamsteed wrote a letter to officials stating that Halley "now talks, swears and drinks brandy like a sea captain" and would be a bad influence on the students. However, thanks to the support of others at the university, Halley got the job in spite of Flamsteed's objections. He was forty-seven years old. Later the same year, he was elected to the Council of the Royal Society; Newton became president.

Once Halley became a full-time academic, his sea expeditions stopped, although he was known as Captain Halley around Oxford until 1710, when he received the degree of doctor of civil law and became Dr. Halley. The title he most cherished, though, seemed to be the nautical one. As a ship's captain, he had been able to put his academic knowledge to practical use.

seven

HALLEY'S COMET

For more than fifteen years, Halley had mulled over the questions raised by the comet he had observed in 1682. Over the years he had tried to calculate its orbit. At first, he mistakenly thought that comets traveled in straight-line paths. Later he deduced that comet paths must be elliptical, like planetary orbits.

When he took up his position in Oxford, and had time to return to his work on the comet, he used a tool that had been unavailable to him before—Newton's *Principia*. These new insights on how gravity worked and tools to measure it opened up new ways to approach the problem. He began to work with fresh tools and new data. The large planets, Jupiter and Saturn, were programmed into his figures, for example. (Uranus, Neptune, and Pluto had not yet been located.)

Halley studied reports of past sightings of comets. He made notes of the date and times recorded. He needed three reliable sources for each comet sighting, from three different geographical positions that could be pinpointed in reference to the stars seen in background vision, to triangulate the comet's position when it was sighted. Many comets were mentioned in old books, but the precise information he needed often times was not.

Tycho and the Comet of 1577

The Dane Tycho Brahe was one of the most colorful figures in astronomy. A wealthy nobleman, he was educated in the finest universities before returning home to begin his career. His family had close relations with the Danish king Frederick II, who granted him use of the island Hven and a generous grant to build the most elaborate observatory ever built.

At Hven, Tycho and his assistants designed and built new observing instruments and dedicated their nights to doing observations. Over a twenty-year period Tycho accumulated the most accurate data available on star positions and planetary motion.

However, one of Tycho's most important discoveries happened almost by accident. He was fishing in a pond late in the day of November 13, 1577, hoping to catch his dinner, when he saw a comet streak across the sky. He rushed to his observatory, where he and his assistants took measurements over the next few days.

Tycho immediately began working on a book on the comet. The book, titled *Stella Caudata*, but often referred to as *The Star with a Tail*, includes details of his observations and measurements of the comet and its path. It became a model for scientific clarity.

In *Stella Caudata*, Tycho demonstrated once and for all that comets originated and traveled well beyond the Moon. The ancient Greek philosopher Aristotle, whose writings formed the basis of what was taught in the universities and churches of Europe, had written that nothing changed beyond the moon. In Aristotles' system, all change was contained in the sublunar sphere. Beyond that, the ceaseless churning of the elements had stopped. Tycho's work on the comet shattered this idea and was a critical step in the progress of the new science.

When a new king assumed the throne in Denmark, Tycho lost his island observatory. Angry, he traveled to Austria and then to Bohemia to serve in the court of the Hapsburg rulers of the Holy Roman Empire. There, shortly before he died, he hired the young German Johannes Kepler as an assistant. Upon his death, the wealth of data he had gathered was handed over to Kepler, who used it to develop the three laws of planetary motion that were so critical to the work of Isaac Newton and Edmond Halley.

Tycho Brahe wrote about the comet of 1577, depicted in this woodcut as it passed over Prague, in his book Stella Caudata. (Courtesy of the Department of Prints and Drawings of the Zentralibibliothek, Zurich)

Tycho Brahe

Halley began by sifting through more than two thousand comet sightings. He searched for similarities in any of the figures before him. He then used the collected data to calculate the orbits of recorded comets. Each comet he studied required pages of calculations.

Halley wrote to observatories throughout Europe, asking them to send him any measurements they had in their own files. Almost everyone cooperated—only John Flamsteed refused. Once he and Halley had been friends, but the rift between them had deepened as Halley's reputation grew.

A detail from a seventeenth-century German woodcut broadsheet depicting the appearance of a great comet.

Finally, Halley appealed to Newton to act as go-between to gather Flamsteed's records. Newton eventually succeeded and presented Flamsteed's findings to Halley, though not until much of Halley's research had already been accomplished.

There were several pieces of information Halley needed. One was the direction comets traveled across the sky. The Great Comet of 1682 revolved around the sun in a *retrograde path*, which was the opposite direction from how the planets and most comets orbit. He discovered that the comets of 1531 and 1607 were also on a retrograde path.

The second thing Halley wanted to investigate was the angle at which a comet approached the sun—how sharply it slanted through the plane of orbits of Earth and the other known planets. That slant is called the *inclination to the ecliptic.* No one had thought to consider this factor as a way of identifying individual comets.

In 1705, Halley finally finished the work he had started in 1695. He had calculated the orbit of every comet that could be accurately placed in the sky, described by three positions against the background of known stars. He had found that there was enough data from only twenty-four of the comets to be used in the study. There was one in 1337, another in 1472, eight from the 1500s, and fourteen from the 1600s. This was a magnificent achievement, but it still was not enough to prove that their courses of motion were related. He had piles and piles of calculations, however, and decided to publish a complete graph describing these twenty-four comets so that, at the very least, the next generation of scientists could recognize new comets or recurring ones.

By this point, Halley was reasonably certain that the Great Comet of 1682 had previously appeared. One of the reasons was because of its retrograde motion. He discussed his theory that the 1682 comet would return on a regular schedule with members of the Royal Society. Then, in 1705, at age forty-nine, he was ready to put his prediction in writing. It was unlikely he would live to verify if he was right himself, but he knew future astronomers would be able to, if they knew what to look for. Not only his reputation as a scholar, but also his claim to immortality was on the line.

Halley encouraged others to check his figures. A French mathematician, Alexis Clairant, and two assistants spent six months going over them. One assistant claimed that the exacting work had damaged his health. The other assistant, a thirty-four-year-old woman, must have had a stronger constitution because she never complained. Their figures matched Halley's, with only a month's difference in the predicted time of the comet's reappearance—a remarkably small discrepancy considering the predicted seventy-six-year gap between appearances.

Following his publication of the work, titled *Synopsis of the Astronomy of Comets*, Halley received many honors. When the second edition of Newton's *Principia* was printed, it included a list compiled by Halley of every single recorded observation of the Great Comet. Records came from Venice, the East Indies, and the English colony of "Maryland, one of the confines of Virginia." No other astronomer could match Halley's understanding of comets.

Now that Halley's prediction about the Great Comet had been made public, the subject was again put on hold. It would take many years to see if he was right. He turned his attention to translating several books of ancient Greek geometry into English. He also discovered a valuable text written in Arabic, and learned enough of the language to translate it into English.

From 1713 to 1721, Halley again edited the work of the Royal Society. The organization continued to grow by adding distinguished members. It became the most-prestigious scientific organization in the world. Scientists in every European nation read its journal. Across the ocean in the new American colonies, professors at Harvard and Yale used issues of the journal as textbooks.

While working for the Royal Society again, Halley had another run-in with an old rival. Flamsteed was always tardy in making his reports public and hesitant to release his

Flamsteed House was the home of the first Royal Astronomer, John Flamsteed, and the heart of the Royal Observatory.

findings to the public. But the Greenwich Observatory had been founded to collect data and to share it, not to hoard it. The king ordered his Royal Astronomer to present his latest findings. Flamsteed ignored the order at first, and when he finally delivered part of his work, it was not complete. With Newton's approval, Halley ordered it published anyway. Halley added his own charts and graphs wherever figures were missing.

Flamsteed was furious at Halley's interference. One letter that Halley wrote to Flamsteed indicates he had been patient, and had sent Flamsteed copies of the manuscript before it went to press. When Flamsteed complained that the work was not finished, Halley agreed to make any changes Flamsteed asked for, promising that errors would be noted and any sheets reprinted if necessary. His letter went on to say:

> Pray govern your passion, and when you have seen and considered what I have done for you, you may perhaps think I deserve at your hands a much better treatment than you for a long time have been pleased to bestow on Your quondam friend, and not yet profligate enemy (as you call me).

Heated arguments between scientists were fairly common. Halley had been dragged into the battle between Isaac Newton and G.A. von Leibnitz, another brilliant mathematician, over who invented calculus, or what Newton called his "method of fluxions." Leibnitz's calculus was being widely used in Europe, but Newton claimed he had created it first, and a controversy erupted that few members of the Royal Society were able to avoid.

As best Halley could tell, both men had come to their conclusions quite independently, but Newton had done so

G.A. von Leibnitz

first. Characteristically, he had not bothered to share it with the scientific community at large, which resulted in his priority being challenged. It was a bitter fight in which Newton exhibited his vast talent for infighting and his willingness to go to just about any length to win.

1910 Appearance of Halley's Comet

"I came in with Halley's Comet in 1835. It is coming again next year (1910), and I expect to go out with it. It will be the greatest disappointment of my life if I don't go out with Halley's Comet."
— Mark Twain

Mark Twain was born during Halley's Comet's appearance in 1835. Seventy five years later, as he predicted, he died when the comet appeared again in 1910. Twain's remarkable prediction and death were not all that was significant about the 1910 appearance of the comet.

1910 marked the first time that photographic equipment was available during the comet's appearance, and the first of Halley's comet were taken then.

Mark Twain

The 1910 appearance also aroused a general hysteria in the population. Many people connected the comet's appearance to religious prophecies, and feared that the comet's appearance was a signal of the end of the world. The belief that comets were harbingers of doom was nothing new. In 79 A.D. the sighting of a comet was blamed for the eruption of Mount Vesuvius, and in 1665, a comet was blamed for bringing the Black Plague to England.

Panic increased when word reached newspapers that the comet's tail contained the poisonous chemical cyanide. People were convinced that when the earth passed through the comet's tail they would be poisoned, even though scientists assured them there wasn't enough of the chemical to do anyone any harm. Some entrepreneurs even began selling medicines they claimed would protect people from the gas. Others sold comet insurance. For days, the comet captivated the public's attention, dominating newspaper headlines and inspiring hysteria.

In the ensuing years, panics related to comet appearances were not as frequent—thanks in no small part to growing public awareness of the science of comets. However, the panic brought on by Halley's comet in 1910 illustrates how deeply people feared celestial events.

eight

ROYAL ASTRONOMER

Once he was no longer clerk of the Royal Society, Halley could be reinstated as a Fellow of the Society, and had more time to spend on his own research. Using some of the research Newton had published in Optiks, Halley returned to a paper he had once written analyzing rainbows and explaining the internal reflection within individual raindrops. He followed this with a study of mock suns and halos, both of which are due to ice crystals in the atmosphere.

He had frequently observed eclipses of the sun and had noticed the irregular edges of the sun when the intense glare was darkened. The pearly colored, sometimes fringelike edge, which can only be seen during a total eclipse, puzzled him. We now call it the corona and know that is part of the gaseous envelope which surrounds the sun, but at the beginning of the eighteenth century no one knew whether the fuzzy circumference was part of the sun or a thin atmosphere surrounding the moon.

Halley also turned his attention back to the stars, where he had begun his astronomical career. He studied in detail the ancient records of Ptolemy and the figures of Hipparchos, who had observed these same stars centuries earlier, and discovered that the early star positions of three of the brightest stars, Arcturus, Procyon, and Sirius, were different from the positions Halley had recorded with his own observations. He concluded that the fixed stars were not fixed at all, but in fact had a motion of their own. This was a novel idea. We know now that the reason movement could not be detected in other

Parallax

Parallax is the apparent shift in an object's position that occurs when the observer is in a different vantage point. It is one of the primary ways we detect distance.

The farther away an object, the smaller the detected shift in position. When the universe was thought to be finite the lack of detectable stellar parallax was used as evidence against the theory that the earth was in motion. If our planet orbited the sun, it was argued, surely the stars would change in size and luminosity as our position relative to individual stars changed. Earth orbited the sun. In reality, stellar parallax was difficult to detect because the universe is infinite, and the stars are at what was then an unimaginable distance away.

Even after the heliocentric model of the solar system was accepted, stellar parallax had not be detected. The world had to wait until telescopes sensitive enough to pick up on the slightest change in position were developed. Finally, in 1838, the German Frederick Bessel announced that he had a shift in position of approximately one-third of a arc second in the star 61 Cygni. (An arc second is one-sixtieth of an arc minute, which is one-sixtieth of a degree.) Over the next weeks, two other astronomers also reported they had also verified stellar parallax of two separate stars.

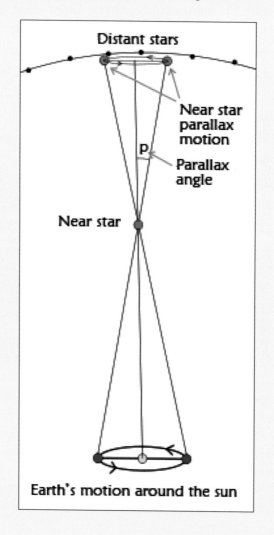

Distant stars

Near star parallax motion

P

Parallax angle

Near star

Earth's motion around the sun

Frederick Bessel

parts of the heavens was because the distance was so great that it was impossible to detect from Earth with the naked eye or basic telescopes. The distance is so great that even if stars were moving in space, the motion could not be seen in one lifetime of calculation. Halley was continuing to add knowledge to the scientific world even in his later years.

John Flamsteed died on December 31, 1719. His work was still unfinished. There was little question of who would be his replacement. Halley, who had earned the respect of his fellow scientists, was the logical choice. He and his wife moved to the Royal Astronomer's house in Greenwich, where Halley found the observatory completely bare. Flamsteed's widow had removed all the astronomical instruments as well as all the furniture. When he protested, she reminded him that her husband had paid for them from his rather meager wages. Halley set about replacing items with a five hundred pounds grant from the royal treasury.

John Harrison

As Royal Astronomer, Halley carried on a wide array of observations. He continued to observe unusual nebulae, fuzzy patches of light in the sky that are now known to be clusters of stars, or other galaxies and variable stars. But his first priority was to complete the map of the changing position of the moon against the background of known stars over an eighteen-year period. This period is called the saros, and is the cycle of motions the earth, moon, and sun pass through as they return to their same positions relative to one another every eighteen years. One of Halley's goals was to use this information in developing a more accurate way to determine longitude at sea.

Soon, however, a man named John Harrison visited Greenwich to show Halley his new invention—a clock that would keep perfect Greenwich time. Keeping time while at sea had always been a stumbling block because pendulum clocks aboard a swaying ship were not accurate. But using Harrison's version of a clock, a sailor could compare Greenwich time with the time at sea. When looking at the North Star at sea, for instance, a sailor would first record the angle and distance from the horizon with charts of what someone would be seeing at the exact same time at the Greenwich Observatory, and compute the ship's longitude.

Halley helped Harrison borrow money to make a working model of the clock, originally called a marine chronometer, although it would make Halley's work on the eighteen-year position of the moon obsolete. Furthermore, he praised the new invention as an important step ahead in future astronomical science. Once again he showed his willingness to help others make scientific progress at his own expense.

Halley continued to write papers on celestial phenomena. One such topic was an aurora, or crown of light, he had observed and realized was purely an optical effect of perspective. His explanation was surprisingly modern. He suggested that aurorae were formed by a luminous "medium" from below the earth's crust and governed by the earth's magnetic field. This we now know to be true, but at the time it was shocking to suggest that a land-based phenomenon such as magnetism could explain a celestial occurrence.

Halley's most important paper in 1720 was connected to his study of stellar parallax. In it, he investigated the question of whether the universe was finite. Some had suggested that if the stars were infinite in number, the night sky should appear as bright as daylight. Halley argued that the brightness of a star's light would depend on how close it was to Earth, and that there was no way we could see farther into space than the rather weak telescopes of his day permitted. He also claimed that because of the law of gravity, everything in space would be attracted to a center point, and the universe would eventually collapse. There were flaws in some of Halley's argument, but it showed his pioneer thinking.

Halley's last years were productive and apparently contented. Then, on January 30, 1736, Mary Halley, with whom Halley had shared fifty-five years "in great contentment," died. She was buried in a churchyard a little more than a mile from the observatory.

Later that same year, Halley seems to have suffered a stroke, leaving him with a slight paralysis in his right hand. He still continued his work with telescopes, but for the first time he needed an assistant to accurately adjust the instruments. James Bradley, a noted astronomer and teacher, came up to

London weekly to help. Halley even spoke of retiring and having Bradley take over the position of Royal Astronomer, but his resignation was declined.

In June 1736, Halley drew up his will, bequeathing almost all his money to his daughters Margaret and Katherine, to be divided equally between them. He considered his son well provided for with his job of "Service to the Crown as a Surgeon." He left a large part of his real estate to his son, but only gave him a modest sum of twenty pounds for "mourning." Tragically, Halley's son died at Gosport, near Plymouth, a year before his father passed away.

While Halley's own health deteriorated, his humor never left him. As medicine, his doctor had prescribed a bitter gruel laced with Jesuit's bark from Peru that contained quinine. In protest, Halley called it his afternoon chocolate, a fashionable drink of the era, and offered it to any guest who might be unlucky enough to drop by at dosage time.

Halley's judgment and memory remained unclouded. He remained an active observer until his death on January 14, 1742, a few weeks after his eighty-fifth birthday. He died peacefully while sitting in a comfortable chair, shortly after enjoying a glass of wine. He was buried in the churchyard at Lee, alongside his wife Mary.

His daughters erected a handsome tomb. The epitaph engraved in stone read:

> Under this marble peacefully rests, with his beloved wife, Edmundus Halleius, L.L.D., unquestionably the greatest astronomer of his age. But to conceive an adequate knowledge of the excellencies of this great man, the reader much have the recourse to his writings: in which almost all sciences are in the most beautiful and perspicacious manner illustrated

and improved. As when living, he was so highly esteemed by his countrymen, gratitude requires that his memory should be respected by posterity. To the memory of the best of parents their affectionate daughters have erected this monument in the year 1742.

In 1854, the original tombstone was moved to the Observatory at Greenwich, where it was set into a wall.

Halley had known he would not live to see if his prediction about the return of the Great Comet was correct. He had also been aware that the date he gave for the comet's return, 1758, was only approximate because the orbit of the comet would constantly be controlled by the gravitational pull of the planets—notably Jupiter—and he could not be sure he had accurate figures for each. But he would have been proud of the accuracy of his figures. The comet's return was first seen by a German farmer and amateur astronomer Georg Palitzsch, on Christmas Day 1758, but astronomers sometimes count the return date as the moment the comet came closest to the

Portrait of the Comet

In March 1986, Halley's Comet flew closer to Earth than it ever had before. Five spacecraft—two Soviet, two Japanese, and one from the European Space Agency (ESA)—were sent to examine it. The ESA satellite, Giotto, flew to within 360 miles of its nucleus carrying ten instruments, including multicolor cameras, mass spectrometers, a dust impact detector, plasma instruments, energetic particle analyzer, and a magnetometer.

Thanks to the information gathered by Giotto, we now have an up-close portrait of the comet. The three regions of Halley's Comet are its nucleus, coma, and tail.

The nucleus consists primarily of water ice and solid carbon monoxide, with additional small quantities of carbon monoxide, methane, ammonia, nitrogen, formaldehyde, and hydrogen cyanide. The nucleus is about six kilometers long and three kilometers in width and depth, making it

Dust tail

Ion tail

Coma

equivalent in size to a gouged-out, flying Manhattan Island. The nuclear surface is a dark, sooty black with extremely low light reflectance (albedo). In fact, comet nuclei are among the darkest objects in the solar system.

The coma is a spherical cloud of gas and dust. It is the main portion of the comet that can be seen by observers.

The tail of the comet extends outward from the nucleus, always pointing away from the sun. Thus, as a comet approaches the sun, its tail extends behind it. As a comet completes its closest approach and begins to sweep back toward the outer solar system, the tail leads the way. A comet's tail may be millions of kilometers long.

The surface of Halley's Comet is very irregular, described by some as resembling a huge peanut shell with hills and valleys of moderate depth. The nucleus is highly porous. Jets of expanding gas shoot out from about 20 percent of the surface at a rate of twenty-five tons per second when the comet is closest to the sun. These jets cause a comet's flight path to vary with quick starts and slow downs as it approaches and leaves the sun. It is only when the sun warms the surface of the comet that the ices turn into gases that leave the comet with explosive force, just as a jet airplane's engine propels the aircraft forward at top speeds.

Instruments aboard the satellites revealed that the comet is 80 percent water ice. Carbon monoxide and dust are additional components. The dust consists of silicates, light elements (sodium, magnesium, sulfur), and a mix of carbon, hydrogen, oxygen and nitrogen. It is important to note that the proportion of carbon in the comet matches that in the sun and other stars, which leads

scientists to believe that comets are remnants of the very early solar system. They possess the various chemical components that, under perfect conditions, may have brought life to our Earth at the beginning of time.

A great deal has been learned about comets since Halley's life, of course. The current theory is that comets formed slowly as grain after grain of matter clumped together. Some of these particles were organic materials from long-gone exploding suns. The clumps of matter floated throughout the galaxy until they became irradiated by cosmic radiation and collided with other grains and eventually massed together into comets. One grain might have received its carbon from a supernova five billion years ago, and another grain came from a red giant someplace else. Comets are composed of diverse particles, and any visiting comet now carries with it the signature of our entire galaxy. Scientists are trying to translate their origin to find the real history of our universe.

Another spectacular feature of Halley's Comet is its fiery tail. A bow shock region nearly a million miles in front of the nucleus is caused by the first interaction with the solar wind. Pressure builds up magnetic field lines in front of the nucleus, and solar wind and ions floating behind the comet head produce a long tail. The tail is what reflects sunlight, giving it the appearance of a flaming sword in the sky. In fact, the word "comet" comes from the Greek word meaning "hairy."

The most recent appearance of Halley's Comet occurred in 1986, but it started its downward path toward the sun in 1948 when it was still in outer space, at a distance computed to be thirty-five times the distance between Earth and sun. In 1970, it drew near to Neptune, the most remote of the great planets. During 1981–84 it passed in front of the Milky Way. By 1985, it had swooped to the heart of the solar system. It swung around the sun in 1986, displaying its tail, and then it climbed out of sight.

In 2061 the comet will pass even closer to Earth, and in 2137 the viewing will be one of the best seen in several millennia.

HALLEY'S COMET

sun (perihelion) on April 13, 1759. Halley's prediction had been remarkably close for a journey that took the comet to the edge of our solar system and back.

To honor Halley's pursuit of scientific truth, the comet was named after him.

Halley's posthumous contributions to science continued. In 1761, the transit of Venus across the face of the sun was observed from a total of sixty-two observing stations, using techniques Halley had developed in 1716. A similar number of observing stations monitored a similar transit in 1769, and the combined results of all these measurements were used to work out the actual distance from the earth to the sun. Halley made his last major contribution to astronomy twenty-seven years after he died.

Timeline

1656   Born October 29 in Haggerstown, England, north of London.

1658   Charles II restored to throne; bubonic plague in England.

1665   Father's apprentice teaches him writing and "armithmetique."

1666   Great Fire of London

1671   Attends St. Paul's School; appointed captain.

1672   Mother dies; measures magnetic compass variations at St. Paul's.

1674   Writes to John Flamsteed, Royal Astronomer.

1675   Sails to St. Helena to observe southern skies; publishes *The Catalog of the Southern Skies*.

1677   Granted Oxford degree.

1678   Elected Fellow of the Royal Society and visits Hevelius in Danzig, Poland.

1680   Tours France and Italy.

1682	Marries Mary Tooke; establishes home and small observatory at Islington; studies comet.
1684	Consults with Isaac Newton; father is murdered.
1685	Appointed clerk of the Royal Society.
1688	Two daughters are born.
1691	Refused professorship at Oxford; studies archaeology to date Caesar's landing in England.
1693	Designs diving bell and helmet to be able to salvage sunken treasure.
1696	Becomes deputy controller of mint at Chester.
1698	Peter the Great of Russia visits England and consults Halley.
1699	Captain of ship *Paramore;* studies variations of magnetic compass.
1701	Checks on harbor fortifications and surveys ports.
1704	Appointed to Savilian professor at Oxford; honored with degree of doctor of law.
1705	Makes prediction that Great Comet of 1682 will return in 1758.
1713-1721	Secretary to the Royal Society.

1714	Calculates exact position of track of shadow of total eclipse due in 1715.
1720	Appointed Royal Astronomer succeeding John Flamsteed.
1736	Mary, his wife, dies; Halley has a stroke.
1737	Right hand affected by paralysis.
1741	Son Edmond Halley dies.
1742	Halley dies at age 86.

Sources

CHAPTER ONE: Ambition and Genius

p. 19, "He not only excelled . . ." Colin A. Ronan, *Edmond Halley, Genius in Eclipse (*Garden City, NY: Doubleday & Co., Inc. 1969) 5.

p. 20, "from my tenderest youth . . ." Ibid., 10.

CHAPTER TWO: Night Sky

p. 23, "He had at this time . . ." Ronan, *Edmond Halley*, 8.

p. 28, "confide to one minute . . ." Ibid., 25.

p. 28, "observed anything of . . ." Ibid.

p. 30, "as a specimen of my . . ." Ibid., 26.

p. 38, "condition of performing any . . ." Ibid., 42.

CHAPTER THREE: Friends and Enemies

p. 43, "You will find . . ." Ronan, *Edmond Halley*, 51.

p. 46, "to converse with . . . " Ibid., 59.

p. 46, "Edmond Halley, his Booke . . ." Linda Walvoord Girard, *Earth, Sea, and Sky: The Work of Edmond Halley* (Niles, IL: Albert Whitman & Co., 1985) 9.

p. 51, "A young lady . . ." Ronan, *Edmond Halley*, 64.

CHAPTER FOUR: The Royal Society

p. 57, "the position of the . . ." Ronan, *Edmond Halley*, 70.

p. 61, "'tho it be 20 fathoms . . ." Ibid., 103.

p. 61, "hott and effete . . ." Ibid., 104.

p. 61, "When we lett down . . . " Ibid.

p. 61, "I have kept . . ." Ibid.

p. 62, "well liquored . . ." Ibid., 105.

p. 62, "I can unlade . . ." Ibid.

p. 62, "bear the hard . . . " Ibid., 98.

p. 63, "1/345,560 part . . ." Ibid.

CHAPTER FIVE: Newton and Beyond

p. 74, "In the publication of this . . ." Ronan, *Edmond Halley*, 86.

p. 74, "It may be justly . . ." Ibid., 86.

p. 77, "For my part . . ." Ibid., 221.

p. 79, "I guess wee shall . . ." Ibid., 157.

CHAPTER SIX: Captain Halley

p. 84, "Instructions for proceeding . . ." Ronan, *Edmond Halley*, 163.

p. 84, "without too much deviation," Ibid.

p. 84, "or as many . . . " Ibid., 164.

p. 86, "On the fifth . . ." Ibid., 167.

p. 86, "being all flatt . . ." Ibid., 172

p. 91, "out of the secret . . ." Ibid., 185.

CHAPTER SEVEN: Halley's Comet

p. 101, "Pray govern your . . ." Ronan, Edmond Halley, 192.

CHAPTER EIGHT: Royal Astronomer

p. 111, "Under this marble . . ." Ronan, Edmond Halley, 214.

Bibliography

Arny, Thomas T. *Explorations*. St. Louis, MO: Mosby
Year Book, 1994.

Calder, Nigel. *The Comet is Coming*. New York: The Viking
Press, 1980.

Christianson, Gale E. *Edwin Hubble, Mariner of the
Nebulae*. New York: Farrar, Straus and Giroux,1995.

Ferris, Yimothy. *The Whole Shebang*. New York: Simon &
Schuster, 1997.

Flaste, Richard, Holycomb B.,Noble, Walter Sullivan and
John N. Wilford. *The New York Times Guide to the
Return of Halley's Comet*. New York, NY: Times
Books, 1985.

Gallant, Roy A. *National Geographic Picture Atlas of Our
Universe*. Edited by Margaret Sedeen. Washington, DC:
National Geographic Society, 1980.

Girard, Linda Walvoord. *Earth, Sea, and Sky: The work of
Edmond Halley*. Niles, Ill.: Albert Whitman & Co., 1985.

Gribbin, John, and Mary Gribbin. *Halley in 90 Minutes*.

London: Constable & Company Ltd., 1997.

Goldsmith, Donald. *The Astronomers.* New York: St. Martin's Press, 1991.

Gorst, Martin. *Measuring Eternity, The Search for the Beginning of Time.* New York: Broadway Books, 2001.

Heckart, Barbara Hooper. *Edmond Halley, The Man and His Comet.* Chicago: Children's Press, 1984.

Levy, David M. *Comets: Creators and Destroyers.* New York, NY: Touchstone Books, 1998.

Marsh, Carole. *Asteroids, Comets, and Meteors.* New York: Twenty-First Century Books, 1996.

Ronan, Colin A. *Edmond Halley, Genius in Eclipse.* Garden City, NY: Doubleday & Co., 1969.

Web sites

The Royal Society
http://www.royalsoc.ac.uk/
This is the Web site of the Royal Society, which is still a functioning body today. Site features a detailed history of the Society and its members, copies of the Royal Society journals, updates about contemporary science, and science-related discussion forums.

European Space Agency
http://www.esa.int/esaSC/120392_index_0_m.html
Information from the European Space Agency about Giotto spacecraft mission, which photographed the nucleus of Halley's comet in 1985.

NASA
www.nasa.gov
the official Web site of NASA (National Aeronautics and Space Administration) features much information about astronomy and space travel, as well as numerous links to other informative sites.

http://photojournal.jpl.nasa.gov/target/Other
More images of various comets and asteroids, found on the NASA website.

http://www.solarviews.com/eng/halley.htm
This site offers numerous images and factoids about Halley's comet.

http://neo.jpl.nasa.gov/images/halley.html
An interesting Web site offering many images of Halley's comet, many of which come from the Giotto.

.

Index